THE STORY OF TITLES

By the same author

The Genealogist's Encyclopedia
The Middle Sea: A History of the Mediterranean
The House of Wavell
The Stuarts of Traquair
Trace Your Ancestors
They Came With the Conqueror
The Golden Book of the Coronation
The Story of the Peerage
Tales of the British Aristocracy
Teach Yourself Heraldry and Genealogy
The Twilight of Monarchy
Princes of Wales
A Guide to Titles
The House of Constantine
Your Family Tree
*Ramshackledom: a Critical Appraisement
  of the Establishment*
*American Origins: A Handbook of
  Genealogical Sources Throughout Europe*
Heirs of the Conqueror
*Heraldry, Ancestry and Titles: Questions
  and Answers*
The Story of Surnames
Tradition and Custom in Modern Britain
The Story of Heraldry
*After Their Blood: A Survey of British
  Field Sports*

The Story of
TITLES

L. G. PINE

B.A. LOND., F.S.A. scot.,
F.J.I., F.A.M.S., F.R.G.S.
Barrister-at-Law, Inner Temple

CHARLES E. TUTTLE COMPANY
Rutland, Vermont

Representatives
Continental Europe: BOXERBOOKS, INC., *Zurich*
Canada: M. G. HURTIG LTD., *Edmonton*

Published by the Charles E. Tuttle Company, Inc.
of Rutland, Vermont & Tokyo, Japan
with editorial offices at
Suido l-chome, 2-6, Bunkyo-ku, Tokyo, Japan
© 1969 by L. G. Pine
All rights reserved
Standard Book No. 8048 0718 3
First Tuttle edition published 1970

Printed in Great Britain

Contents

1. Introductory

(Ptolemy V) . . . 'living for ever, beloved of Ptah, God Manifest . . . son of God and Goddess, like unto Horus, son of Isis and Osiris.' *The Legacy of Rome* (1957), p 50.

'Son of the great master, the god of the earth and the sky.' Title of African king in what is now Southern Rhodesia, in the tenth century AD. *A Short History of Africa*, by Roland Oliver & J. D. Fage (1962), p 48.

'Muy grande e y poderoso Senor, hijo del Sol, tu solo eres Senor! todo el mundo te oya en verdad.' Description of the Inca of Peru, quoted by W. H. Prescott in *The Conquest of Peru*, Everyman Edition (1907), p 603.

'Father and Pastor, Pope and Patriarch, Father of Fathers, Pastor of Pastors, Bishop of Bishops, Thirteenth Apostle, Judge of the Universe.' Title of the Greek Patriarch of Alexandria, in *The Papacy*, A. L. Maycock (Benn, 1927), p 4.

The above are examples, which it would be possible to extend almost indefinitely, of the titles borne by monarchs in Africa and in South America, dating from the centuries before Christ up to the sixteenth century AD, and including the style now used by a high ecclesiastic of the Greek Orthodox or Eastern Church. There is a remarkable, though quite unrelated resemblance between the styles of monarchs in the Old and the New World; there is the ascription of divine sonship as with the former Emperors of China, and even now with the present Emperor of Japan. The term commonly used in the West—Mikado—is rarely employed by the Japanese. To them, their Emperor is Tenshi (Son of Heaven), Tenno (Heavenly King), Dairi (Court), Gotho (Palace), Aramikami (Incarnate God), Akitsukame (Manifest Destiny), and so on, in a plethora of royal terms. From such oriental hyperbole and, to us, superfluity of titles, some blasphemous to any Christian or theist, it may seem a sharp descent to occidental realism when we read the beginning of the letters patent which create a baron of the United Kingdom : 'Elizabeth the Second by the Grace of God . . . To all Lords Spiritual and Temporal and all other Our Subjects whatsoever to whom these Presents shall come Greeting Know Ye that We of Our especial grace certain knowledge and mere motion do by these Presents advance create and prefer Our trusty and well beloved A . . . B . . . Esquire to the state degree style dignity and honour of Baron X . . . to have and to hold unto him and the heirs male of his body lawfully begotten . . .' etc. etc.

Yet behind this comparatively simple formula there is a vast and intricate structure of titles. Dukes, marquesses, earls, viscounts and barons each have their particular styles of address, written and spoken. There are numerous other classes of titles and each represents a survival in Britain of what was once universal. It was calculated by the Abbé Sieyès that in France at the end of the eighteenth century there were 110,000 noblemen. In Continental countries all members of a noble family are noble, and though titles have ceased to be created in almost every European country except Britain, the wide-spreading branches of nobility make it well nigh impossible to record all those still in existence. Even now, without the creation of fresh titles in European lands, multitudes of counts, barons and princes survive. There are in the world today over twenty independent monarchies. Formerly, these were always accompanied by lower hierarchies of title, and it is only within the present century that a halt has been called to the making of titles. The 1914-18 war saw the fall of three great monarchies of Russia, Germany and Austria, and the end to any fresh recruitment to the phalanx of nobles which had surrounded those august thrones. Even monarchies which survived the catalclysm of two world wars, as in the Low Countries and in Scandinavia, have ceased to create new nobility. The strongly Socialistic spirit of Sweden for one has refused to countenance any addition to its nobility since the time of Sven Hedin, the explorer, in 1903, and the former House of Nobles now stands in Stockholm mainly as a place of interest to the heraldic antiquary and the tourist.

It would be misleading to suggest that the cessation of title-making over most of the world has meant the triumph of democratic outlook. Monarchies have been replaced by republics, often termed in their official parlance, People's Republics. Over one-third of the

8

human race from the shores of the Pacific to the centre of Europe now comes under the rule of dictatorships, and in these Communist-dominated states there is not even equality in misery, certainly not in status or title. The Comrade General or Comrade Commissar possesses powers far beyond those of his counterpart in the government of democratic states. The adulation given to Mao Tse-tung in China cannot be equalled save in the annals of the Roman or Chinese emperors.

Even in democratic lands the absence of the constitutionally conferred title has meant the substitution of the self-granted honour. Americans by their constitution may not use titles of nobility, but this has not prevented American ladies, of whom Princess Grace (Kelly) of Monaco is a charming example, from marrying titled husbands and thus acquiring a handle to their names more attractive than plain 'Mrs.' General Dwight Eisenhower could accept only an honorary knighthood of the Order of the British Empire but his countrymen are not deterred from membership of organisations which, within their ranks, recognise a strict gradation of title. American Masonry, for example, is much more variegated in its official styles than its British counterpart. America is also the ideal country for the genealogist and herald, who will there find far greater support than in Europe; earnest seekers are always endeavouring to prove their descent from Norman conquerors, Magna Carta barons, and knights and ladies of the Order of the Garter. Heraldry flourishes in America in three distinct ways. It seeks recognition from the Court of St James, via the College of Arms, by direct grant; it has set up its own organisation of bodies which record and grant arms;* it is the instrument of charlatans and frauds who offer arms and pedigrees drawn from books to people who are merely namesakes of some notable family. In Canada, Australia and New Zealand, too, there is a growing interest in genealogy and heraldry, which is inseparable from title and which confers on the successful researcher into his origins a feeling of elevation above the general mass. In South Africa there is even official provision for a state herald, though perhaps not surprisingly in view of that country's racialist philosophy of white supremacy.

If then, even now, the yearning for title continues to find expression in many ways—*naturam expellas furca tamen usque recurret*—it is but further evidence of the universal interest there has always

* For American College of Arms, see note at end of chapter.

9

been in titles. It is a phenomenon found all over the world wherever civilisation has appeared, and found, too, in semi-civilised or savage communities. It is primarily due to a human frailty, the longing for recognition. Hilaire Belloc once wrote that the desire for fame was almost extinguished in some holy men, and deadened in many unholy men, but that it could easily be revived in the latter. Desire for title is a desire for fame : to be distinguished among one's fellows. An inherited title will also confer distinction, and since a woman usually takes her husband's title and rank (from Majesty to Mister) we must not forget the considerable influence of women in this sphere.

There is, then, in titles an element at once creditable and discreditable. Good in so far as desire for distinction may bring out fine qualities in a man. He may use his talents to better purpose if he hopes for Sirdom or Lordship as a result. Bad, in that the pursuit of honorific distinctions can lead a man to lying and bribery, and even worse, to trampling on those who get in his way. Whether laudable or reprehensible, however, the desire for honours is a universal feature of human life, and if not satisfied by a direct system, as in Britain, it will find an outlet in some other way. Even where an honours system does function, there will still be complaint, since only a few persons in a nation can hope for recognition, though in Britain we seem to have reached a solution by practical rule-of-thumb methods, as we so often do. Our system of honours has been broadened, so that many more people now come within its purview, and at the same time much of the old feudal spirit has been allowed to depart. Several orders of chivalry which became obsolete with the rapid eclipse of the British Empire are no longer bestowed. The Order of St Patrick lost its significance with the separation of the twenty-six counties of southern Ireland from the British Crown, and the independence of India relegated to limbo the Orders of the Indian Empire and of the Crown of India. No longer do the ranks of the peerage receive dukedoms and marquessates outside the royal family and its connections; very few baronets were created between 1945 and 1951, and no honours list has included baronetcies or hereditary peerages since 1964. Parallel with these changes there has been a growth in non-hereditary honours, and these have been conferred on persons from more and more varied spheres.

It could well be that we are witnessing the disappearance of title in the old feudal sense, and if it goes in Britain, it is unlikely to flourish elsewhere. A large number of old titles will still persist, but these will slowly dwindle, since there will be no fresh recruitment to them; and it will grow ever more difficult to check those that remain in foreign lands as no official records would be kept. Already it is impossible to know if a Continental countship or other noble title is genuine. The *Almanach de Gotha*, after nearly two centuries of life and after surviving the French Revolution, Napoleon and the first world war, fell a victim to the Russians in the second. No work has replaced it, and for reference purposes we are thrown upon the records of the various national societies which try to keep up the supply of information. Even such bodies as these are not permitted to exist in the lands behind the Iron Curtain and for one-third of mankind we have no up-to-date information on their old titled ranks. When we reflect that the Dalai Lama of Tibet is an exile and that the last Emperor of China was a brain-washed gardener in Pekin, we can appreciate the futility of trying to trace the fate of any titled persons or their honours within the Communist-controlled third of the world.

Modern attempts by democratic states to emulate the British system of honours, have been, at least, poorly conceived and directed, and the resultant titles, as with a Kentucky colonelcy, do not survive the holder. Except for a tiny trickle of traffickers in bogus orders, and their dupes, none of the substitutes for the courtly rigmarole of the past makes even a pretence at continuity beyond the life of an individual recipient. Yet only sixty years ago the existence of great imperial and regal systems of honours was an accepted fact. As with everything else in this century, the change has been of unprecedented rapidity and, for this reason alone, it is of interest to seize and record the details of the swiftly disappearing romantic past. Within only a few decades anyone bearing a princely or ducal title will seem like a hangover from *The Prisoner of Zenda* —as though an actor in an historical romance had strayed into a real life street scene still wearing his stage clothes.

Certainly the old titles made for colour in what might otherwise have been a world as drab and undistinguished as our own. When they have all gone—and soon many holders will relinquish their titles or suffer their honours to slip into obscurity behind a plain pseudonym of Mister—we shall all be alike and even greater will be the monotony of a machine-dominated and materialistic way of life which some future Toynbee will no doubt flatter with the title of a civilisation. The prospect is as little attractive as the older system, harsh and insensitive as it was behind its superficial glamour.

In 1898, when Alfred Russell Wallace wrote his book, *The Wonderful Century*, Britain was the world's leading power; the British Empire was the greatest in history, uniting a quarter of the earth's surface in a rule of peace and justice; Europe was the Queen of Continents; white supremacy prevailed everywhere, save in resurgent Japan; western civilisation, the product of the ancient classical cultures of Greece and Rome, cleansed, invigorated and cemented by Christianity, had spread over the whole world, the first civilisation so to do. There was much poverty, misery and ill health beneath the magnificent structure; but there was boundless hope in the possibility of man's progress, and a growing freedom. Then came the catastrophe of world war in 1914. From that, and the failure to achieve a lasting peace after 1918, derive all our ills. Our immense progress in physical science unaccompanied by moral or spiritual growth means either that we face the nightmare of impending destruction or the indefinite prospect of an uneasy truce, ever bordering on actual warfare, between the most powerful states. In the meantime the proliferation of machinery never stops and, with rare exceptions, individual life becomes standardised in an ever fiercer chase after more expensive cars, refrigerators and television sets, and in the pursuit of sexual experience. It may help, then, to look back to a simpler, more human and attractive age. Certainly it will not harm anyone to catalogue and meditate upon the names which men and women have thought reasonable to have bestowed upon them : Holiness, Majesty, Highness, Lord, are epithets of the Supreme Being, as well as titles applied to men.

NOTE : American College of Arms. Since this book was prepared, the writer has received full information about the organisation in Baltimore, Maryland, which has been established under the above heading, in order to register, confirm or grant arms to Americans. This body, which is staffed by officers thoroughly learned in heraldic science, has already made sufficient progress to have granted arms to ex-President Lyndon Johnson, President Richard Nixon and Vice-President Spiro Agnew. Its establishment opens up great possibilities for the future of a true American heraldry.

2. The Origin of Titles in the Mediterranean World

The foundations of our civilisation are Roman. We derive our institutions and our legal codes from Roman sources. Our religion comes to us from the Latin world. This origin of our modern western way of life from the Roman Empire is no less apparent in the sphere of title. We can hardly refer to any form of title—imperial, regal, noble or patrician—without being aware that these terms derive from Latin sources. Even when the word is of Greek origin, as with 'monarchy' or 'ecclesiastic', it comes to us through the medium of Latin.

Rome, although making great contributions of her own, owed much of her civilising influence to the Greeks. Inept as the latter were in political life, they excelled in the arts and sciences. *Graecia capta ferum victorem cepit.* The Romans rolled the 200 or so petty Greek states into the province of Achaia, and for ever abolished the freedom and political life of Athens, Sparta and Thebes; but the Greeks gave to their new masters philosophy and literature, sculpture and painting. When Aeneas, whom Virgil portrays as the ultimate founder of the Roman race, is conducted through the underworld by the shade of Anchises, the latter proudly consoles Rome for its lesser standing in the arts :

> *Excudent alii spirantia mollius aera*
> *Credo equidem, vivos ducent de marmore vultus;*
> *Orabunt causas melius, coelique meatus*
> *Describent radio, et surgentia sidera.*
> *Tu regere imperio populos, Romane, memento*
> *Hae tibi erunt artes: pacisque imponere morem.*
> *Parcere subjectis et debellare superbos.*
>
> (*Aeneid* VI, 847 seq.).

Let others mould marble into living likenesses, plead more eloquently or show a greater skill in scientific exposition. The Roman's peculiar skill lay in the art of government.

Both Roman and Greek, none the less, owed much to earlier civilisations in the Near and Middle East. Perhaps the Greeks never forget their respect for Egyptian achievement. They and the whole of western civilisation received great benefits from the oriental empires which preceded the conquests of Alexander the Great. Sumer and Akkad, Babylon and Assyria had, like Egypt, known millennia of history and greatness before the Greeks had emerged from the pre-Homeric age. When we turn the pages of the Old Testament, we read of the great king, the King of Assyria; or again of one so lofty in his majesty, the King of Persia, that his style of king required no adjective before it. The Old Testament is full of kings and lords, and it is not therefore surprising that the regal title derives from the ancient East. In the Authorised Version of the Bible, the English word 'king' is applied to persons who differ very greatly in status and importance but can be classed together in one respect, that they have supreme power in their particular community.

The term 'king' is of the most ancient origin in English, being found in Old English as *cyning*, while similar words occur in the languages to which English is allied, German, Swedish and Old Norse. In those languages it means the head of the race, or clan, who is its father, and a reputed descendant of the gods. If we look at the pedigree of the Kings of Wessex as given in the *Anglo-Saxon Chronicle* we shall find, along with a dexterous linking with the genealogies of the book of Genesis, an ascription of regal descent from the old pagan Saxon gods. The same phenomenon appeared in most of the western genealogies, Celtic or Scandinavian, Welsh or Germanic. A fiction similar to the belief that the king was literally the father of his people lies at the root of the genealogies of the Scottish clans. Theoretically, Macdonalds, Mackenzies, Macphersons, etc are all akin; in fact, nothing could be further from the truth. The genealogy of the clan chief shows his descent from the reputed founder of the race; there are numerous junior branches, but in every generation many men and their families would come under the protection of the chief and therefore bear the clan name.

Considering, then, the great discrepancy between, say, the thirty-and-one kings of various towns in Canaan, whom Joshua slew, and the mighty sovereign of the book of Esther, Ahasuerus 'which reigned from India even unto Ethiopia, over an hundred and seven and twenty provinces', considering this enormous disparity in power and authority, it was natural for the Greeks, the first Europeans to visit the Orient, to differentiate between the Persian monarch and the rest. They used the term ὁ ἄναξ for a lord or ruler; ὁ βασιλεύς for a king or chief; for the King of Persia, the word βασιλεύς was employed, but generally without the article, or if the article was used, 'great' was added ὁ μέγας βασιλεύς. It is interesting that this over-riding impression of the Persian sovereign's greatness appears after the Persian wars in which the tiny states of Greece had decisively defeated the Persian Empire. Though triumphant, the Greeks had still a very profound respect for a dominion which terminated three or four months' march from the Aegean, if indeed they could envisage a boundary of any sort for it. In consequence of this estimation of the position of the Great King, the term βασιλεύς began to acquire a meaning far higher than that of our word 'king'. It came to be equated with that of 'emperor', so that Alexander and his generals, who after his early death subdivided his empire, were styled kings but in a different sense from the little rulers of Sparta. Later still, when the Greeks and all the other Mediterranean peoples had become subjects of Rome, the word βασιλεύς was applied to the Roman emperors. As we shall see, in a later chapter, this Greek word was to have a usage and peculiar meaning for English kings before the Norman Conquest. It is worth noting that in nineteenth-century Europe a king who achieved special power, or whose country achieved great influence, was rarely content with his ancestral regal style. Queen Victoria in 1877 became Empress of India; the King of Prussia in 1871 was proclaimed Emperor of Germany; and for six or seven years in the late 1930s the King of Italy was styled Emperor of Ethiopia.

The eastern style was always magniloquent, and it was common usage for the greatest sovereign (for the time being) to set his foot on the necks of those kings whom he graciously allowed to live. The placing of the foot on the neck of lesser monarchs was more often actual than metaphorical, and plenty of monuments survive which show the vanquished or the vassals before their conqueror or overlord. In one such monument, Jehu, King of Israel, is depicted as kneeling to kiss the feet of Shalmaneser of Assyria. It was a rare compassion indeed which moved Evil-Marodach of Babylon to take

15

Jehoiachin, King of Judah, out of prison and make him a pensionary of the royal household. Even so, we read in this story of the kings who were with Evil-Merodach in Babylon, poor dethroned vassals, being kept at court so that they might not make trouble elsewhere for their master.

Little wonder that the supreme rulers of these eastern empires took to themselves titles which to us savour of the grossest presumption and of blasphemy. 'King of Kings' can be applied only to One Being, yet this style is frequent in the old empires of the Fertile Crescent, the only palliation of the offensive usage being that the eastern potentates considered themselves either as descended from the gods, and thus semi-divine, or else as favourites of the deities. The term for the ruler of Egypt, the Pharaoh, meant originally, 'great house' (thus exhibiting an affinity with the Japanese terms for their emperor), but the Pharaoh was spoken and thought of as Son of Ra, the sun god. The royal house of the Pharaohs being divine, it could not marry outside its own ranks, hence the alliances of brothers and sisters in marriage. When Egypt fell to the lot of one of Alexander's generals, Ptolemy, the latter's descendants adopted not only the style of the native monarchs but, in course of time, their habit of intermarriage in their own families.

Only perhaps in modern Ethiopia does a survival of this style continue, in the Emperor of Ethiopia's title of King of the Kings of Ethiopia, though the use of the article before 'kings' does imply a great difference from the ancient King of Kings.

For many ages the styles, titles and observances of the oriental rulers had immense influence. Clearly, if a divine personage was on the throne he must be approached with profound homage. Prostration was the accepted mode of obeisance before the Persian king. When the famous Athenian statesman, Themistocles, was exiled from his country, he decided to try his fortune at the Persian court. He was warned that he could not approach the King's presence as the Greeks were wont to do, but that he must prostrate himself. This he did, and was duly rewarded with the King's confidence and rich presents. Another indication of the awful majesty of the Persian monarch occurs in the story of Esther who, although she is Queen of Persia, yet risks her life by coming unbidden into the royal presence.

With the style and title, European successors of the Persian king took over his attributes of divinity and claimed the extreme sub-

16

servience shown in approaching him. Alexander the Great began his career as King of Macedon, where a race of hard-fighting, hard-hunting, and hard-drinking soldiers tolerated the position of *primus inter pares* in their king. He ended by adopting the robes and habits of the Persian whom he had replaced, and even his European friends were expected to prostrate themselves before him. To be plain son of Philip of Macedon was not enough; Alexander had to be divine and saluted as son of Zeus by the oracle in the oasis of Ammon. He certainly exhibited all the caprices of the worst deity in the pagan pantheon. His successors were like him and assumed the styles of the oriental lands which they governed. In Egypt the Ptolemies, as noted above, took on a distinctly Pharaonic appearance. The Seleucids who secured Babylonia and many other lands from the Aegean to the Punjab were orientalised from the first. One of their most notorious members was Antiochus IV Epiphanes. He tried to convert the Jews from the strict monotheism of their religion to the worship of the Greek Olympian Zeus, with whom Antiochus himself was identified. The result was the Maccabean war with the short-lived emergence of Israel once more as a monarchy, to be followed by its subjugation by Rome. When the great Emathian conqueror tried to extract the same adoration from his Greek as from his Persian subjects, the Macedonian soldiers' objection to this oriental usage was ultimately the cause of the death of one of Alexander's closest friends, Clitus, whom the Great King killed with his own hand.

The welter of weak kingdoms and empires ruled over by Alexander's διάδοχοι, or successors, lasted in steadily declining strength for some 200 years, their collapse waiting only on the appearance of a great and vigorous power in the Mediterranean world. In the second century BC such a legatee of greatness came forward in the Roman Republic. Oswald Spengler, in one of those brilliant passages which illuminate the dark unintelligibility of much of his *Die Untergang des Abenlandes*, says that after the battle of Zama (202 BC) which terminated the Second Punic War, Rome conquered through lack of opposition, for there was no more Roman vigour. Like most generalisations this cannot sustain examination. The conquest of Gaul, of Spain, came in the last age of the Republic, that of Britain in the first century of the Empire. No lack of vigour here, but with reference to the Asiatic and Egyptian powers Spengler's remarks are justified. When the Romans first encountered the

17

Seleucid monarch, Antiochus Epiphanes, in 190-189 BC, they were ignorant of the weakness of their opponents. They chose their army with great care, and while the force was commanded by Lucius Scipio and Gaius Laelius, the consuls of the year, they had with them Publius Cornelius Scipio (the brother of Lucius Scipio) who, in an unofficial capacity, was to be consulted by the consuls throughout the campaign. Publius Cornelius Scipio bore the additional name, or rather title, of Africanus because he had gained victory at Zama and conquered the terrible Hannibal.

Here the original Roman idea of title should be noted. While most other nations were content without surnames, the logical and precise Roman mind worked out a system of nomenclature. Normally a Roman had three names; the *praenomen*, corresponding to our 'forename' (a literal translation of *praenomen*); then came the *nomen*, or clan or race name. This latter was the name of the *gens*, or gentile name; in the case of the famous Publius Cornelius Scipio, his middle name denoted that he belonged to the *gens Cornelia*. Last came the *cognomen*, or surname, which was used to denote the different families of the same race. Thus Marcus Tullius Cicero; or Gaius Julius Caesar of the great patrician *gens Julia*, whose *cognomen*, Caesar, was that of an ancient branch of the *gens*, race or clan. It is important to realise this, because the surname of Julius Caesar eventually passed into a title. As Dr Cyril Alington remarks : 'The fact that great rulers such as Kaisers, Tzars and Shahs have been proud to bear the name of a simple Roman family is a dramatic evidence of the impression which Caesar made upon the world.' (*Europe*, 1946, p 11.) It is also amusing, as Dr Alington went on to point out, that the first supreme ruler of the Roman world could have borne another surname, and to speculate on what titles would have then been made from Cato, Cicero or Brutus.

Starting, then, from this precise Roman system of names, we can go on to study developments of the Roman titular system which was built around their nomenclature. When a man had distinguished himself in the service of the state he was honoured in various ways, and often by receiving a title. Thus Scipio had been given the title of Africanus, and, again, after he had forced Antiochus Epiphanes into a peace which definitely lowered his status, Scipio received the additional title of Asiaticus. This is a distinct parallel to the British custom whereby a successful general is granted a title which incorporates the name of his greatest victory. Thus we have Viscount

18

Montgomery of Alamein, Earl Kitchener of Khartoum, Baron Napier of Magdala, and many others, including even the fictitious positioning of Plassey in county Clare, when an Irish peerage was conferred on Robert Clive for his great victory at Plassey, in Bengal, in 1757. Moreover, just as such titles descend in our peerage families so, too, branches of the Roman patrician lines were distinguished by an *agnomen* often derived from an ancestor's title conferred by the Republic, so that we have a branch of the Scipios, Scipio Africanus, Asiaticus etc. From this habit in ancient Republican Rome eventually developed much of our western titular edifice.

When the first Roman campaign in Asia had been easily successful, the Levant was gradually brought within the sphere of Roman influence. Within 200 years of Africanus' having gained his second title of Asiaticus, the whole of the Eastern Mediterranean world had come within the Roman Empire, either ruled directly or as client, vassal states. Thus when Christ came to be born, the Jews of Palestine, like other Roman subjects, were bound to conform to the decrees of Caesar Augustus.

The confrontation of Roman and Eastern which then took place had far-reaching consequences for Rome. No longer was poverty or simplicity the mark of the Roman. He had become immersed in the habits of the luxury-loving, sycophantic orientals. The contemplation of eastern adulation before a monarch might at first excite contempt in Roman minds, but unconsciously they were influenced. The last century of the Roman Republic was an age in which great subjects became over great for the safety of the state. Marius, Sulla, Crassus and Pompey all took advantage of the weakness and corruption of the Roman government to build up a personal authority and following. Finally, all the rival generals were overcome by the greatest of them, Caesar. He assumed purple robes, whereas previously a successful Roman politician had been content with the purple-bordered robe of a consul. He accepted the right to wear always in public the laurel crown. He became Dictator for life (a precedent to have serious consequences 1,800 years later in France), and began to call himself *Imperator*, which meant, simply, 'commander-in-chief' and as such was the designation of the holder of an independent command *(imperium)*. It was the custom after a great victory for the soldiers to hail their general as an *imperator*, or true general, who had proved himself in his command, and the title could also be conferred upon a general by the senate. When

19

Cicero was proconsul of Cilicia he campaigned against the robber tribes of Mount Amanus and, for his successes, was given the title of *Imperator*. However, Julius Caesar intended his assumption of the title to be permanent. It was taken over by his adopted son, and gradually came to form part of the name of the Roman rulers, thus contributing the title of emperor to the world.

It was some time before the steadily growing influence of the east took full effect in Rome. Augustus, the first emperor if we omit Julius Caesar, was careful to preserve the forms of a republic but his successors, over the course of a century, advanced ever closer to the assumption of absolute monarchy. Not only this, but the oriental poison almost unconsciously imbibed led them to the conception of their own divinity.

NOTE: The origin of the Roman titled system. Plutarch, in his life of Pompey, refers to the bestowal by the senate of the title of 'Magnus' on Pompey when he was only twenty-four years of age. He goes on: 'In this connexion one cannot help feeling respect and admiration for the ancient Romans: these titles and surnames of theirs were not only given as a reward for successes in war or in military leadership; achievements in civil life and the abilities of statesmen were also honoured by them.' (Plutarch, *Fall of the Roman Republic, Six Lives*, translated by Rex Warner, 1958, p 150.) In the same passage, Plutarch gives two examples of the bestowal of 'Maximus', or 'The Greatest', on two men for non-military services. There is also the famous case of Quintus Fabius Maximus who was surnamed 'Cunctator', or 'Delayer', because by his proverbially Fabian tactics he had foiled Hannibal after the latter's great victory at Cannae in 216 BC. How far the name 'Cunctator' (Ennius quoted by Cicero, *unus homo nobis cunctando restituit rem*), was a nickname retained as a surname or was a title of honour, is not entirely clear. It appears to have been the former. It is, however, an interesting point that in the great Fabian *gens*, many of the various families bore the surname of Maximus. At least five families were of the Maximus branch. This *gens* claimed descent from Hercules and a daughter of Evander of Arcadia. Most of the great *gentes* of Republican Rome asserted similar descent from the old gods and goddesses, the *gens Julia* being sprung from Venus, an analogy, as we shall see, with the pedigrees of the ruling families in western Europe in the Dark Ages. Probably some early member of the Fabian *gens* received the title of Maximus and this was handed on in the various branches as the titles of Africanus or Asiaticus were with the Scipios. Here, then, is the germ of our own titled system in Britain, with distinctions which became hereditary.

20

3. The Development of Titles in the Roman Empire

Julius Caesar is usually reckoned as the founder of the Roman Imperial system, but not formally as the first of the emperors. He intended to make a clean sweep of the old republic. It was rumoured that he even meditated adopting the title most abhorrent to a Roman—that of *rex* or king. This possibility has been made familiar to us by Shakespeare's play; there was a contemporary oracle which proclaimed that the Parthians could be conquered only by a Roman king. At the time of his death in 44 BC, Caesar was said to be contemplating an expedition against the Parthians who, nine years before, had inflicted a humiliating defeat upon the Romans under the generalship of the multi-millionaire Crassus. Hence, perhaps, the inspiration of the oracle. Whatever the facts about Caesar's eastern projects, any plans were terminated by his bloody end in the Senate House in Rome.

Thirteen years later Caesar's grandnephew and adopted son had become sole ruler of the Roman world. In the expressive saying of Tacitus—*postquam bellatum apud Actium atque omnem potentiam ad unum conferri pacis interfuit* : after the battle of Actium, when all power had come into one man's hand, there was peace. (*Historiae*, i.c.l.)

The new Julius Caesar was the son of Atia, the daughter of Julia, and herself the sister of the great Dictator. Atia married Caius Octavius, of whose origin various stories were circulated by the Roman gossip writers but who had, in fact, an honourable career. He was governor of Macedonia in 60 BC, and died suddenly in Campania the following year, when his son, the future emperor, was only four years old. It may be noted that the elder Octavius had gained some military successes and been hailed as an *Imperator*, so very ordinary was the original use of the term from which our

21

word 'emperor' has come. The four-year-old boy was named after his father, Caius Octavius and, in accordance with Roman custom, when he was adopted by Julius Caesar he called himself Caius Julius Caesar Octavianus. After he had obtained supreme power, the name Octavianus ceased to be used and in a short time the new Caesar acquired a fresh name and title, that of Augustus, by which he has become known to history. This was in 27 BC, when Munatius Plancus proposed in the senate that the name should be given to Caesar in recognition of his service to the state, and is the year which some historians regard as marking the beginning of the Roman Empire.

From this time, too, there date a number of titles acquired by Augustus, and these have become familiar over the centuries in usages which, while preserving the names, have departed greatly from their first meanings. Augustus, unlike his adopted father, made no attempt to destroy the old Roman institutions. He preserved the senate and while, in theory, he handed over his powers to the sovereign people, everyone knew that he remained the great power in the Roman state; hence a grateful senate and people regranted him his prerogatives for life. There was no suggestion of a revival of the term 'Dictator'. Had it been applied to Augustus it is quite probable that it might have been used in subsequent ages instead of *Imperator*. As it is, 'Dictator' remained what it was originally, the designation of a supreme autocratic ruler responsible to none. Until the present century there were few instances of dictatorship, and very few, if any, in which the actual name has been used. In our time, of course, the dictators have been numerous in many parts of the world, and the word has almost always carried with it the pejorative association which Augustus knew his countrymen disliked. His assumption of titles was carefully designed to reflect his own supremacy while avoiding injury to Roman susceptibility.

The first title borne by Augustus was that of Imperator and expressed what we might call his power in foreign and external affairs. He was commander-in-chief of the armies and dealt with all matters of policy external to the Empire. But this was not the limit of his powers, and to signify these he chose the term *Princeps*—or prince, a word destined to last to the present time. This title of *Princeps*, or chief, could be derived from the expression, *Princeps civitatis* or prince of the Roman citizens. It could also come from the *Princeps senatus*, or prince of the senate, though the latter

22

opinion is not generally held. *Princeps senatus* was the senator whose name was first on the list and who had the right to give his opinion first. Here, as with the tracing of emperor from the military term *imperator,* we have a word which has acquired a meaning quite different from its primary usage.

The basis of Augustus' power was in the Roman people, not the senate, and while he would certainly wish to be known as head of the senators, the term *princeps* would cover both the senatorial position and that derived from the popular will. It enabled Augustus to play the game of equality with the senate, which is sometimes known as the Dyarchy. This dualism refers to the double rule of emperor and senate. Gradually, as the first century of the empire passed, the system tilted in favour of the emperor.

It was only after much careful consideration that Augustus decided to assume the title of *princeps*. He had first thought of using a title derived from his tenure of the office of consul, a term describing the position of the two principal magistrates of the old republic who had been initiated in 509 BC after the expulsion of the kings. These magistrates were elected annually, and as they had equal powers it was thought that this arrangement would prevent any development of tyranny. They had equal rights of command in the field and, if they commanded together, they took it in turns day by day to act as generals. When, at the end of the third century BC, the Romans acquired their first possessions outside Italy, it was quite natural that the retiring consuls should undertake the government of the new provinces, acting on behalf of the newly elected consuls. A consul after laying down his office would become *pro consule,* a proconsul responsible for the administration of a province. Thus Julius Caesar, on ceasing to be consul, received the proconsular province of Cis Alpine Gaul, Gaul this (ie, Roman) side of the Alps. In addition, he was given the territory of Transalpine Gaul and, as everyone knows, during his tenure of the proconsulship he conquered Gaul, so establishing his powers as a general and his ability to recruit an army.*

Augustus was consul in 27 BC and saw to it that he was re-elected each year for the next four years. In practice, however, he found that there were awkward features in the holding of a perpetual consulship, not least that he had a colleague who was legally equal to him. His thoughts then turned to the tribunate. The office of

* See Note 1 on the office of consul at the end of this chapter.

tribune had been instituted in 494 BC during the quarrels between patricians and plebeians, in order to protect the people from the nobles. Ten tribunes were elected annually, and veto by any one of them could prevent a bill from becoming law. Augustus had the tribunician power *(tribunicia potestas)* for life, but this still did not give him all that he wanted and eventually he adopted the somewhat ambiguous title of *princeps*, destined to live on for 2,000 years, to express his position. That it was ambiguous there could be no doubt, which was why Augustus deliberately chose it. Under no circumstances would he use the title of *rex*. Not for him the forthright and sweeping changes which would have expressed the genius of his adopted father. Augustus would have been at home within the useful hypocrisies of the English political system, but whereas the House of Windsor has lost all its real prerogatives while preserving all the titles of monarchy, the Roman imperial system maintained the forms of the republican past but grew steadily into an absolutist monarchy. After three centuries the rulers of the Empire were lonely eminences, absolute in power over their subjects provided that they could control their armies. To the very end of the western empire—the official date for its fall is 476—the forms of election were gone through with senate and consuls, though all real power had for long rested with the *princeps*.

Imperator and *princeps* are, then, the origin of our familiar emperor and prince, and other Roman offices have also contributed their share of title to the modern world. Consul is so much in use today that it requires a special note. Proconsul has never been a modern title but has been frequently used in modern English to describe the governors sent from England to rule large provinces of the former British Empire. It was a literary and popular usage to speak of someone like the late Lord Lugard as a great proconsul, but it was never a formal title except, of all places, in the very lowest grade of the British consular service! It was also applied by English writers to distinguished colonial governors in the French Empire, such as Marshal Lyautey of Morocco. Even more extensive has been the use of the term 'tribune'. The original tribunate having been created for the protection of the people, it has been regarded as essentially democratic and the words 'tribune of the people' have been applied to all manner of persons (and newspapers!). Perhaps the most curious of these latter usages is the title of the American *Herald Tribune*. No office could be more emblematic of feudal

24

authority than that of a herald, and its union with the idea behind the word 'tribune' is a tribute to transatlantic word-play. 'Tribune' is usually employed in a popular sense, rather than as a formal title, though in the fourteenth century, during the brief revival of the Roman Republic under Rienzi, the latter was designated as Tribune of Rome.

Another office under the old Republic was that of censor, which was always held by someone of consular rank. The original duty of the two censors was to hold the census, or reckoning, of the Roman people, but many other duties came to be attached to the office. The censors had the task of revising the list of senators and of the *equites*, or knights, and inevitably this carried with it the power of moral discrimination and the use of what we have come to describe as censorial powers. One of the most interesting episodes in the history of the Roman censorship is the tenure of the post by the famous Marcius Porcius Cato. He was elected censor in 184 BC and carried out his work with such great severity that he was given the *cognomen* of Censorius. In our days he would have been regarded as ultra-conservative (or, if I may use slang, as the squarest of the squares) for he was opposed to all innovations as being likely to corrupt the old Roman way of life. In this he was right but, like most people who struggle against an incoming tide, his efforts were destined to fail.*

The full title of the first of the Roman emperors deserves close study because of its importance as a forerunner of many modern titles, and because it gave rise to such important changes in later times in the empire. Augustus in the last year of his reign—AD 14— had as his full title : *Imperator Caesar Divi Filius Augustus Pontifex Maximus, Consul xiii, Imperator xx Tribunicia Potestate xxxvii, Pater Patriae*. The last resounding term was conferred upon him by the senate at the end of his life. It has not been borne as a regular title in modern times, though it has been used in connection with the names of prominent patriots, eg, George Washington. *Imperator* has already been described, here the Roman *princeps* has accepted the homage of his troops by including among his titles the number of times they had saluted him as a true general. In the same way, Augustus added the number of occasions on which he had been elected consul or had received the tribunician power.

Pontifex Maximus was used to denote that Augustus was head

* See Note 2 on Censor and Censorship.

25

of the state religion. This title could have died with the worship of the old gods; instead, as we shall see, it became one of the principal styles borne by the head of the spiritual Roman Empire, destined to sway regions Caesar never knew. The name Caesar, as already remarked, was the family name of the great Dictator, a family which had prolific progeny. Our own Kaisar-i-Hind, once borne by British sovereigns, derives from it. Augustus was used by the emperors as the senior title. Finally with the changes introduced by the Emperor Diocletian, there could be more than one Augustus at the same time, and more than one Caesar presiding over divisions of the empire.

With the term *Divi filius* we reach one of the strangest riddles in connection with titles borne by human beings. 'The son of a god'. Of what god? As Augustus was the adopted son of Julius Caesar, the reference is, of course, to the latter. Listen to a most sober historian of the scientific school on this matter. 'He [Julius Caesar] had permitted himself to be worshipped as a god, during his lifetime; and though no building was set apart for his worship, his statue was set up in the temples of the gods, and he had a *flamen* of his own.' (J. B. Bury, *Roman Empire*, 1893, p 16.) Caesar died at the age of fifty-seven but until he was over forty, he was known simply as a Roman politician, little better than others of that ilk, a man of fashion and a runner-up of colossal debts. Within the space of fifteen years, from this unpromising material developed a great general and ruler of men, and one who permitted himself to be worshipped in his lifetime. There was nothing in the Roman tradition to suggest such an advancement. True, Romulus, the titular founder of Rome, after his mysterious death, had become the god Quirinus, but there were no other instances of deification in the history of the republic, and certainly no case of a living man who received divine honours. The vast success of Julius Caesar in becoming the sole and effective master of the Roman world may very well have turned his brain, and, indeed, Major-General J. C. Fuller, in his study of Caesar, concluded that he was not always responsible for his actions. Some of Caesar's admirers may try to palliate the astonishing blasphemy of his acceptance of worship by arguing that he thus intended to convey to the Romans that an entirely new era in their affairs had begun. When a good clergyman like S. Baring Gould writes admiringly of Julius Caesar, it is noticeable that he maintains a judicious silence on the subject of the Dictator's deity, yet it was an amazing

26

action for a professed atheist like Caesar to allow himself to be treated as a god.

Augustus, on the other hand, was far more circumspect than his great uncle as regards divine worship, and in the matter of his titles generally. Julius Caesar, after his murder, was numbered among the gods of Rome, under the title *divus Julius,* by a formal decree of the senate and people. Augustus never received divine honour during his lifetime. He used the style 'son of a god' but his elevation to divinity waited until his death. Then the principle was followed that an emperor had to be judged worthy of divinity by his people, who thus posthumously decided upon his merits. Before a hundred years had passed, an emperor, Domitian, was habitually designated as *dominus ac deus.* Domitian, however, was a tyrant and after his assassination failed to secure the deification which he had bestowed upon himself in his lifetime.

Like Augustus and his predecessors, some of the early emperors were consecrated or deified. Claudius, one of the house of the Caesars, was thus honoured, and so were two of the succeeding Flavian dynasty, Vespasian and his elder son, Titus, the conqueror of the Jews who had destroyed Jerusalem in AD 70. Vespasian was a man of humble Italian farming stock who laughed about the elaborate pedigrees constructed for him by his courtiers. As he was dying, he made a joke about his own approaching apotheosis. *Ut puto deus fio.* 'As I sigh I am made a god.' Nero and Caligula, like Domitian, were never deified.

The ascription of divinity to great rulers was not confined to the Romans. In our time the aura of godhead still lingers around the Emperor of Japan, and the priestly head of Tibet, the Dalai Lama, is regarded as the reincarnation of the first of his line and, as such, a living god. But the number of divine rulers was far greater in the past than it is now. In Egypt, the Pharaohs were 'divine', and in the new world, the same was held true of the Incas of Peru. In these lines of monarchs the race was of heavenly origin; with the matter-of-fact, businesslike Romans, divinity was something put on or off with the office of emperor. Perhaps the theory formulated by Euhemerus in the third century before Christ had something to do with this attitude. He had explained the deities of Greece as glorified men who, like Romulus, had been divinised.

Along with the growing power of the Caesars went a corresponding attitude of reverence from their subjects. It was a serious offence

27

in any way to impugn the position of the emperor, and detection of the crime of *majestas* or treason *(lesè majesté)*, for which the penalty was usually death, was the constant hope of a crowd of *delatores* or informers. The law against treason, *Lex Julia de majestate*, was passed under Augustus, who did not use it unduly, but his adopted son and successor, Tiberius, became suspicious and embittered and encouraged the *delatores*. Succeeding emperors, as they were good or bad, discouraged or encouraged the odious race of informers.

The principle that the emperor was divine evolved like everything else connected with the Roman ruler. In the train of the emperors came a whole succession of gods, goddesses and godlings. The ladies and children of the royal house were granted divinity, and the wives, and sometimes the mothers, of emperors were known as Augusta, by decree of the senate. When Nero divorced his wife and married Poppaea, who had been his mistress, she, too, became Augusta by order of the senate. Nero was overjoyed when she bore him a daughter and when the child died after three months, he insisted upon her being made a goddess. When Poppaea herself died two years later, owing to Nero having kicked her when she was with child, she, too, was divinised.

As might have been expected, the practice of deifying human beings did not stop with the imperial family. The emperor Hadrian had a favourite youth named Antinous who was drowned in the Nile. 'The event excited general sympathy throughout the empire. Hadrian deified his lost favourite, dedicated a temple to him and built Antinoopolis in his honour. Coins were struck with the head of the "Hero Antinous", and his statues were multiplied in the cities of Asia.' (Bury, *op cit* p 507.)

One of the earlier emperors, Gaius (Caligula), the successor of Tiberius, was in the habit of committing incest with his sisters. When one of them, Drusilla, died, he had her deified under the name of Panthea. He exacted worship from his subjects and was furiously offended when the Jews refused to comply. He was murdered in time to prevent a Jewish rebellion, for had he lived it was his intention to force the Jews to sacrifice to him as to a god.

Meditating upon this strange phenomenon of emperor worship, it is easy to understand the persecutions of the early Christians. To the easy-going Romans, it seemed quite natural to offer incense to the statues of the emperors. Whatever could be the matter with these mad people who refused to worship not only divine Caesar but the tutelary deities of Rome? To the uniniated Roman, the Christians must have been classed with the Jews, as a sect of atheists. But the Christians, for their part, had inherited from the Jews the same unbending belief in one God, which it had taken the Chosen People centuries of rough shaping to acquire. From the earliest days of the church, the Christians had worshipped God the Father (the Lord of the Old Testament), who had revealed Himself through His Son Jesus Christ who, after His earthly life, had sent the Holy Spirit to begin the work of the church on the day of Pentecost. Not three Gods, but one God in Trinity. With this robust faith, the early Christians could have no truck with the vanities of the heathen. They were prepared to be faithful subjects of the empire and to pray for the emperor, but never to sacrifice to him or to the gods of Rome. Consequently persecution of Christians by the state was inevitable.

After varying fortunes over 300 years, and ten officially recorded persecutions, the Catholic Church received the imperial peace. Constantine, the first Christian emperor, gave the Christians rest from persecution in the Edict of Milan (AD 313). Eleven years later this was followed by something much warmer and of very far reaching consequences, when Constantine, now become sole emperor, sent out proclamatory letters throughout the Roman world urging all his subjects to follow his example and become Christians. Within a year of having embraced the truth of Christianity, Constantine presided over the first great General Council of the church at Nicea, in 325, but he deferred reception of the sacrament of baptism until he was on his deathbed twelve years after his conversion.

Small wonder that special privileges should have been so readily allowed to the emperor by even the greatest of the Christian bishops. After three centuries in which persecution unto death had alternated in short, painful spasms with longer periods of contemptuous toleration—with times in which the church was able to expand without active or official resistance, allowed to build its own edifices and to hold property—followed in the late third century and the beginning of the fourth century with a tremendous persecution under Diocletian and his successors, now at long last the whole body of Christians could breathe freely and plan its way of life, sure not only of the goodwill of the supreme ruler, but of his participation in the Christian creed and Christian worship. At Nicea, when the bishops assembled for the council, they were saluted by the soldiers at the emperor's command, those same soldiers who would just as readily have arrested and led them to execution at the emperor's command. As Canon Philip Hughes remarked, it must have seemed to the bishops that the Kingdom of God had come indeed.

After all this, it is a shock to recall that Constantine was consecrated by the senate and placed among the gods whom he had renounced. 'The title, the ensigns, the prerogatives of Sovereign Pontiff, which had been instituted by Numa, and assumed by Augustus, were accepted, without hesitation, by seven Christian emperors; who were invested with a more absolute authority over the religion which they had deserted, than over that which they professed.' (Gibbon, ch xxi.) By AD 390 the toleration of Christianity by the state had passed into a prohibition of the pagan religion. Only for two years (361-62) under the emperor Julian (usually known as the Apostate, because he had renounced Christianity) did paganism make any attempt to arrest the Christian triumph.

In the course of the fourth century, the balance of power between Christianity and paganism eventually tilted decisively in favour of the former, but during this time, covering three or four generations, there was inevitably much overlapping between the two religions. It was not until AD 375, when Gratian became emperor, that the position of the Pontifex Maximus was given up. 'The Christian emperors condescended to accept the robe and ensigns, which were appropriated to the office of Supreme Pontiff. But when Gratian ascended the throne, more scrupulous or more enlightened, he sternly rejected these profane symbols.' (Gibbon, ch xxviii). Within a few years even the senate, the last stronghold of paganism in Rome, was coerced or persuaded to give up the gods. The temples were empty and deserted, and soon were used either as converted churches (like the Pantheon at Rome, or the temple of Athene on the Acropolis at Athens), or as quarries for the construction of other buildings.

As the temples were thus abandoned, so one of the titles of the emperors, that of *Pontifex Maximus*, was left without an owner. Like the sword of Captain Greatheart in the *Pilgrim's Progress*, it was free for him who could earn it. Among the other great changes which mark the reign of Constantine is the supersession of Rome as the seat of government. Establishment of the new capital at Constantinople meant that 1,000 miles lay between the Bishop of Rome and his temporal sovereign, the emperor, but it was some

30

time before the Bishop adopted, as the designation of the chief Christian pastor, the title *Pontifex Maximus*. Thus, from the age of Diocletian and Constantine, dates a series of titles destined to live with the empire for a millennium and to bequeath a lasting legacy to the European nations.

NOTE 1 : On the office of consul. We have in this term a striking example of the retention of a word which has altered its meaning. The word 'consul' did not lose its old connotations entirely during the middle ages, when it was used by some of the Italian states to designate their chief magistrates. At the end of the eighteenth century, where there was much study and imitation of Roman history, the term 'consul' was revived in France after the Revolution. In 1799 three consuls were appointed, with Napoleon as First Consul, no doubt on the Orwellian principle that some consuls are more equal than others. Napoleon was in effective control and in 1804, when he became Emperor of the French, the consuls were dropped.

The modern usage of 'consul' is in reference to a man whose duty it is to look after the interests of his fellow citizens abroad. The ancient Greeks had a similar system but with the reverse arrangement in that the man who cared for the interests of foreigners was not himself a foreigner but a native of the state. He was the *proxenos* who, having a natural liking for the particular breed of foreigners, was chosen to act in effect as their consul. One is tempted to reflect that should this method ever be revived in modern Europe, Britain, with her host of citizens who prefer every country to their own, would have no difficulty in discovering a multitude of *proxenoi*. This aside, however, the origins of the modern consulate office, familiar to all, spring from the practice of merchants who elected one of their number to settle their trade disputes. In the Near East, this system was used and extended so that the consul became responsible for the general security of his nationals. It was especially so when dealing with the Moslem states. Until the seventeenth-eighteenth century, the presence of an ambassador was unusual in a European country, that is as a permanent figure. His appearance was usually in connection with a special matter, to arrange a royal marriage, secure a military alliance or settle a particular dispute. The more permanent official, the consul, had the duty of carrying out everyday diplomatic relations. When regular, permanent embassies became established, the diplomatic functions of the consular office declined and reverted rather to those of a commercial nature. In many eastern or African countries consuls and capitulations (concessions in China) went very much together. In the period of European supremacy, many oriental and African powers were persuaded to grant special favours to a western nation, often resulting in that country having its extra-territorial courts and jurisdiction in the host country. This system has now gone, as the non-European world has regained its power.

The British Consular Service has five grades, those of consul-general, consul, vice-consul, consular agent and proconsul.

31

NOTE 2 : In the history of modern Europe the terms censor and censorship have had a history coeval with the beginnings of printing. The first censorship office was started at Mainz in 1486, the birthplace of printing, as though in warning that officialdom did not intend the new invention ever to be free. In the sense of censorship of books, plays, newspapers and suchlike, there has been a history of 500 years' warfare between those who wish to publish or produce freely and those who wish to control them. The most familiar plea in English for the freedom of authorship and the press is that of John Milton, written in 1644, but it was not until the nineteenth century that the press obtained its freedom from various forms of censorship. Even up until 1968, plays in England were censored by the Lord Chamberlain's department, a survival from the times when he used to license troupes of players. Under the Cinematograph Act of 1909 the power to censor films rests with the local authorities, which means that, in the United Kingdom, there are more than 700 local licensing bodies which can control the showing of films. The British film industry also has its own voluntary system of censorship, represented by The Board of Film Censors, which consists of a president, whose appointment must be ratified by the Home Secretary, a secretary and several viewers. Some authorities in Europe have a system of state censorship of films, but in the USA, a body popularly known as the Hays Office and set up by the film industry, acts as censor. Apart from these obvious instances of the use of what was an ancient Roman title, there is also the usage, known to all who have served in the armed forces during the two world wars, of censorship of letters, and also in the civilian sphere of censorship of letters and newspapers.

4. The Eastern Roman Empire

Between AD 284 and 285 the Roman empire came under the rule of a person of low birth, the son of a manumitted slave, who possessed the highest ability in affairs both military and political. This was the emperor Diocletian. He perceived that the constant pressure of the barbarians on the frontiers of the empire, and the commotions caused by ambitious generals seeking to make themselves emperors, made government by a sole ruler so difficult that it was bound to break down. He therefore associated with himself in the supreme power one of his colleagues, Maximian. Presently two younger generals, Galerius and Constantius, were appointed as Caesars, the two seniors being known as Augusti. These four divided the provinces of the empire, and each was supreme in his own jurisdiction. They were colleagues, not rivals. Diocletian also used Milan rather than Rome as the seat of his government, an example followed in an even more momentous change some forty years later when Constantine made his new capital the chief city of the empire.

In the matter of title, Diocletian wrought great and far-reaching changes. For nearly 200 years the fiction had been maintained that the emperor was a magistrate, and the term *'Princeps'* had been used to ease the transition to an absolute monarchy. Inevitably, the title of *Dominus*, or Lord, was added; inevitably, because of the reality of the emperor's power and through his ascription of divinity. Although Roman prejudice prevented the use of *Rex*, the styles of the emperors were apt to pass into the language of hyperbole. *Divinitas, numen*, sacred majesty, divine oracle, were terms employed of, and often by, these rulers. The inhabitants of the eastern provinces of the empire, accustomed to the styles of oriental monarchy, readily applied them to the emperors. The term βασιλεύς, or King, had a much higher significance than that of *Rex*, and having been

a

used of the Persian sovereigns, when it was applied to the emperors, it carried with it an attribution of more than human greatness.

Diocletian introduced an oriental servility into the court life of the empire. He assumed the diadem—a fillet in the form of a ribbon, which was worn round the head and tied at the back; sometimes in Persia bound round the tiara which only the Great King could wear. He wore impressive robes. Access to his person was restricted and when he showed himself to his subjects it was with a magnificence well calculated to instil awe and wonder. He certainly rose to his responsibilities, considering that his name at birth had been Docles, enlarged to Diocles and, finally, to the Roman dignity of Diocletianus.

There followed naturally the creation of a huge crowd of officials, all bearing titles and possessing privileges, who stood between the ruler and the bulk of his subjects. To secure audience of the supreme earthly being, it was not only necessary to make a long and wearisome pilgrimage through these numerous grades of high officials, but also to be prepared for something unheard of in the western world. The subject was compelled to fall prostrate before the throne and to adore the divinity seated thereon. Diocletian had come of hardly peasant stock and had risen to eminence as a soldier, so it is very difficult to understand how he could have allowed the imposition of such servility upon his subjects. No one was exempted from the rule of abject prostration, not even the emperor's oldest military comrades or his highest officers.

The arrangement whereby the empire was administered by two Augusti and two Caesars did not last long. It was a Caesar, Constantine the Great, who reunited the empire after having overcome his colleagues in civil war. But the reunion was short lived. The idea of a division between the eastern and western portions of the empire became accepted, and within a century and a quarter of Constantine's death the two branches had parted company. Only in the sixth century did Justinian try to recover the old dominion. Although he was partially successful, even this recovery did not endure beyond his lifetime. In AD 476 the western empire ended; the eastern, centred on Constantinople, lasted until 1453. Diocletian's reforms had had the effect of removing the natural centre of administration from Rome and, by subdividing the empire, had helped to bring about the disintegration of the Western half.

Meanwhile, the innovations introduced by Diocletian into the titular system and in the worship of the emperor found a permanent home in the Byzantine court. The site which Constantine selected for his new city was at the junction of Europe and Asia, and was certainly of great strategic value, as each succeeding age has shown. Moreover, the emperor was sincere in his Christian profession and felt that, with the founding of a great new city, a start could be made free from the incubus of paganism. A third reason, probably of lesser weight than the others with a man of Constantine's understanding but still of importance, was that a new city would make it easier to extend the Diocletian system of government.

There already existed, as can be imagined, a classification of honours in the Roman state which Constantine accepted and developed. The Romans had used their method of the *cursus honorum* to build up a division of titles. There were then among the Roman magistrates three classes : (i) The Illustrious, which included the consuls and patricians. Under the empire, the former had been degraded from an important office into an honour empty of power but conducive to great expense. The patricians were the ancient order as distinguished from the plebeians, and in the earlier days of republican Rome there had been lengthy disputes between the two orders. Long before the establishment of the Principate, the distinction between patrician and plebeian had ceased to be of importance politically, since plebeian birth formed no bar to the holding of office. The Illustrious also included the prefects of Rome and Constantinople, the generals of the army and the members of what we would call the Cabinet, that is the seven ministers of the palace. (ii) The *Spectabiles*, or Respectables, a title borne by persons who held some rank or position reckoned as higher than that of the senators. Such were the proconsuls of Africa, Achaia, and Asia; such were also the rulers or counts (*Comes*=Count) of the thirteen great dioceses of the empire. The Count of the East was the head of the first diocese. Egypt possessed an Augustal prefect, though the arrangement instituted by Augustus, by which a Roman knight filled the post, no longer prevailed. The other eleven dioceses were ruled by vicars or vice-prefects. Although Byzantine rule has long passed from practical life into the history books, such terms employed in its administration as diocese and vicar have far outlasted their beginnings. Also entitled to the term Respectable were the military counts and dukes whose ranks have also achieved a not inconsiderable longevity. (iii) The *Clarissimi*, or Honourables, was the title accorded by custom to the senators. Under the Byzantine classification, the lesser magistrates or governors of the subdivisions of the provinces received this title.

Many of the terms of reverence or self-glorification borne by the VIPs of modern Europe and America find their origin in the usages of the Byzantine court. 'The principal officers of the empire were saluted, even by the sovereign himself, with the deceitful titles of your Sincerity, your Gravity, your Excellency, your Eminence, your sublime and wonderful Magnitude, your illustrious and magnificent Highness.' (Gibbon, ch xvii.) Excellency has become the style of colonial governors, Eminence has found a home in the Catholic Church, and Highness is, of course, the modern designation of princes of the blood royal, though in past centuries it was applied also to great kings. Thus before the time of Henry VIII, who adopted the style of Majesty, our English sovereigns were addressed as Highness.

Although many European terms of honourable address began in the mazes of Byzantine protocol, their meaning, or application, has since changed very greatly. This is true of the titles of dukes and counts, which were at first purely military titles and not hereditary. 'The titles of counts, and dukes . . . have obtained in modern languages so very different a sense, that the use of them may occasion some surprise. But it should be recollected that the second of those appellations is only a corruption of the Latin word which was indiscriminately applied to any military chief. All these provincial governors were therefore dukes; but no more than ten among them were dignified with the rank of counts or companions, a title of honour, or rather of favour, which had been recently invented in the court of Constantine.' (Gibbon, ch xvii.) The relative rank of a duke and a count has been reversed in western Europe, although these terms were borrowed from the old empire. The count once exercised great powers, and readers of early British history will recollect that official, the *Comes Saxonici littoris*, Count of the Saxon Shore, whose duty it was to protect the English Channel coasts and those of East Anglia from the ravages of the barbarian Saxons.

In addition to the numerous officials mentioned above, there was the imperial cabinet of seven great ministers on whom the emperor conferred the rank of Illustrious. (i) The *praepositus*, or prefect of the royal bedchamber, whom Gibbon in western style terms the Great

Chamberlain. He was a eunuch, yet took precedence over all the *Respectabiles*. (ii) The Master of the Offices, whose position might in some ways be compared with that of a medieval Lord Chancellor. He was the chief magistrate of the palace and to him were addressed appeals from the provinces of the empire, especially appeals in which the ordinary magistrates and courts could not intervene, just as the English Chancellor heard appeals in equity which could not be allowed at common law. (iii) The *quaestor*, one of the offices in old Rome which involved first the management of the finances of the consuls, then of the proconsuls, and in due course of the various provincial commanders. It was a custom of Augustus to select one of the quaestors to read his speeches in the assembly of the senate. The other quaestors were abolished and gradually the sole remaining holder of this ancient title came to be looked upon as the mouthpiece of the council and, in some sense, a source of jurisprudence. (iv) Count of the Sacred Largesses was the title given to the treasurer-general in charge of the revenue. (v) There was also a count who was responsible for the emperor's private estate. (vi) and (vii) The counts of the domestics, or commanders of the household troops, whose duty was to guard the person of the emperor.

It may be noted that the emperor Augustus had distinguished a number of persons among his subjects as his officially styled 'friends'. His closest companions outside his family circle, they were, in fact, the *comites* of the emperor. Hence in later centuries the title of *comes*, or companion. A parallel can be found in the English usage by which the sovereign addresses a duke as his or her cousin. In the fourteenth century, when the title of duke was first created in England, only persons of the blood royal were dukes.

In course of time a labyrinth of ceremonial usages grew up around the Byzantine emperor and his court. The members of the imperial dynasty were said to be *Porphyrogeniti*, or born in the purple, a term originating from the use of the famous Tyrian purple (in Latin, *purpura*.) This was a dye which came from the shellfish *(purpura)*, and as it was very costly to obtain robes of this colour, they were usually appropriated to royalty. Hence perhaps the meaning of the phrase 'born in the purple', denoting the small class of those who were entitled to wear this colour. In the Byzantine empire there was a palace called the Porpyhra at Constantinople, where the imperial ladies were accustomed to retire for their child births. As early as the fourth century the poet Claudian refers to those 'born in

37

the purple', so there may also have been a custom of wrapping the new-born imperial scion in purple-coloured robes. One of the emperors of the tenth century, Constantine, was named expressly *Porphyrogenitus*, perhaps an allusion to his authorship of works dealing with his empire and its administration and ceremonies, an achievement to be expected only from the quintessence of the em-purpled few. The custom, of naming the imperial family thus, had, however, definitely been established before his time.

Purple as a sign of greatness has not disappeared from the modern world; the expression 'Promoted, or raised, to the purple', denotes that the man concerned has been raised to the cardinalate of the Roman Catholic Church, another reminder of the frequent adoption by ecclesiastics of secular terms.

The reigning emperor of the East was further distinguished from the rest of the royal family by the use of the word βασιλειά, derived from βασιλεύς already mentioned and taken to mean Majesty, with which the adjective ἀγιά, holy, or sacred, was often joined. The supreme ruler was thus known as His Sacred Majesty, a curious terms for the orthodox ruler of a Christian state, yet one which has found repetition again and again in the mode of address of the crowned heads of Christendom. English folk will remember the application of 'Sacred Majesty' to the Stuart kings. In the *Eikon Basilike* (written by Charles I, or at least expressing his senti-ments), the more exact title is: 'The Portraiture of His Most Sacred Majesty in His Solitudes and Sufferings.'

John Selden in his enormous work, *Titles of Honour*, refers to the pompous styles of Greek (ie, Eastern Roman) and oriental emperors, and well might anyone be sickened by them. The usages of Augustus and Caesar were long left behind, although, as Gibbon observes (ch liii), those of Caesar had been employed for over 1,000 years to denote the second person in the state. With the advent of the Com-nenian dynasty in the eleventh century, a new series of royal titles began. From the Greek forms for Augustus and Emperor—*Sebastos* and *Autocrator*—a compound was produced, *Sebastocrator*. This person came above the Caesar, and second only to the emperor, though it appears that the term 'Despot', or 'Lord', was also used for the second member of the royal house. The order of the titles given to those born in the purple was therefore, after that of the emperor : (i) Despot; (ii) Sebastocrator; (iii) Caesar; (iv) Panhyper Sebastos and (v) Protosebastos. These were appropriated to the princes of the blood or to their in-laws. Thus the husband of the celebrated Princess Anna Comnena, author of the *Alexiad*, was known as the Caesar Nicephorus Briennius. Of him, Sir Walter Scott observes in his romance, *Count Robert of Paris*, which deals with the time of the First Crusade, that he held '. . . the rank of Caesar, which, however, did not at that period imply, as in early ages, the dignity of second person in the empire. The policy of Alexius had interposed more than one person of condition between the Caesar and his original rights and ranks, which had once been second only to the emperor himself.'

With the increase of the royal titles had also gone a proliferation of those borne by servants of the state, just as the number of high officials in the centralised bureaucracy increased with the contraction of the empire caused by the Islamic conquests. A similar phenomenon has occurred in England with ever increasing hordes of officials housed in ever larger buildings to administer a non-existent empire and dwindling armed forces.

The Greek, or Byzantine, titular system was as follows : (i) The *Protovestiare*, who, as his name implies, was responsible for the wardrobe, but with time came to rule over the palace menials and to preside at the emperor's audiences. (ii) The Great Logothete, who was in charge of the laws and revenues. (iii) Two officials whose names were derived from the Moslems, the Chiauss and the Dragoman (both to have a long history in the oriental world), whose function was to introduce ambassadors. (The word 'dragoman' is familiar to an older world of travellers in the Near East, as meaning an interpreter or guide, especially in Egypt.) (iv) The *Great Domestic*, who was commander-in-chief of the army. (v) The *Protostrator*, who was the equivalent of the Master of the Horse in modern parlance. (vi) The *Stratopedarch*, who was the judge of the camp, perhaps similar to our Judge Advocate General. (vii) The Commander of the Household Troops, who was known as the *Protospathaire*. (viii) The *Konostaulos*, or Constable, who ruled the Frankish mercenaries. (ix) The *Aeteriarch*, who was over the barbarian troops. (x) The *Acolyth*, or Follower, who commanded the Varangian Guard. This last body is of peculiar interest to us, as it was formed from Englishmen who preferred exile to living under the Norman conquerors of their country. As late as the year 1453, a Varangian guard still existed. (See J. M. Neale's novel, *The Fall of Constantinople*.) (xi) The *Great Duke*, who was the commander of the naval forces; under him were the *Great Drumgaire*, and third in command, the *Emir*, a title of Saracen origin, but which, in the form of 'Admiral', is one of the Arabic legacies to Europe.

The Byzantine empire underwent many changes in its millennium of life, reckoning from the year 476. The adjective Byzantine has become synonymous with an involved and slavish bureaucracy equal in tediousness to that of imperial China. Yet it is only now, in the present century, that the immense services of the empire have been properly acknowledged. Had Constantinople fallen 500 years earlier, the greatest Christian state would have been extinguished. Europe was sheltered for many centuries by the empire, and the conversion to Christianity and to civilization of the Slavs (except for the Poles) was due to the missionaries of Byzantium. It is to the eternal discredit of Western Europeans that the Fourth Crusade ruined the eastern empire, and that in the twentieth century, Constantinople—degradingly known as Istanbul—was allowed to remain in Turkish hands.

NOTE: The title of Exarch. This is often mentioned in histories of the later Roman empire, especially with reference to the Exarch and Exarchate of Ravenna. It is derived from two Greek words meaning 'to lead out of', but is really the equivalent of our viceroy. It was of course a title of office, and not hereditary. It has long since ceased to exist politically but like many other terms defunct in the political world, it has acquired an ecclesiastical use. In the eastern or Greek churches, the exarch was (i) the primate of a diocese, (ii) the head of certain monasteries, and, (iii) the deputy of the Patriarch of Constantinople in collecting tribute payable by the church to the Turkish government. In the present time, the exarch is a deputy of the Patriarch, similar to the Roman legate *a latere* whose duty it is to visit an ecclesiastical province.

5. The Early Middle Ages in Western Europe

The date AD 476 is taken by the majority of historians as marking the end, or fall, of the Roman empire in the west of Europe. In that year a boy who had been made nominal emperor, and 'who by a curious irony of history bore the names of the founder of Rome and the founder of the empire' was deposed. (*Shorter Cambridge Medieval History*, vol. 1, p 101.)* A barbarian leader then became the ruler of Italy, as other barbarian chiefs had set themselves over the other provinces of the former empire. The attitude of Odovacar is typical of the awe with which these rude semi-savages still regarded the majesty of Rome, although for a century they had plundered and devastated its fairest provinces and its capital city. 'By his orders, the Roman senate sent a solemn embassy with the imperial insignia to Constantinople, declaring they did not need a separate emperor and begging Zeno (the eastern emperor) to grant to Odovacar as his lieutenant in Italy the title of patrician. Zeno replied with much diplomatic adroitness. He praised the pro-Roman sentiments of Odovacar and conferred on him the title of patrician. . . . The façade of imperial rule was thus maintained.' (*Op cit*, p 101.)

Here is a plain statement in a careful history which agrees with the more detailed and, of course, emotive account by Hilaire Belloc in *Europe and the Faith* (ch iv, 'The Beginning of the Nations'). We are not here concerned to inquire into the Bellocian theory that the fall of the Roman empire never occurred and are interested only in the points he makes about the use of titles by the new barbarian chiefs. He imagines a traveller whose commercial interest has brought him to the centres of local government, eg, Paris, Toledo, Ravenna and Arles. In Spain, he has to get in touch with the local officials and with the actual government. He is directed to the *Palatium*— which, Belloc stressed, ought not to be translated by our 'palace'.

* See note, Ironies of History, at end of chapter.

Palatium was a word derived from the Palatine Hill in Rome, where the early Roman emperors had had their private abode. As they gradually gave up the pretence of being merely the servants of the republic, their private residence became more and more the official seat of government. Here, once more, is an example of the Roman background and foundation of our institutions, in the very words which we use to describe them. We cannot help speaking Latin and using Roman terms.

Continuing with the imaginary traveller in Spain, on reaching the *Palatium* he would have found things much as they had been in the several centuries of direct Roman rule. Affairs were conducted in the name of a single person and of his council. This person would use the insignia (at least on important official occasions) of a Roman governor, such as the orb and sceptre held by the latter as representative of the emperor. There were two great differences, however, between the ruler of the fifth or sixth century and the Roman governor of earlier times. He was known as *Rex*, which we usually translate as 'King', but which meant rather 'chieftain' of a tribe and then, later, denoted the local ruler. This *Rex* was surrounded by a council of great landowners, the forerunners of the feudalism which is the distinguishing mark of medieval civilization. Incidentally, our word 'nation' derives from the Latin *natio*, but in classical usage *natio* always denotes a tribe and never has the meaning of our 'nation'. With the titular centre of authority as far away as Constantinople, it can easily be understood that the links which connected the local ruler with the emperor grew steadily weaker. Under Justinian (527-65), a very strenuous effort was made to recover the western provinces. Great as this was, it never got beyond the shores of the Mediterranean, taking in all the north African coast, Italy, Sicily and the other western Mediterranean islands, and a little of southeast Spain. Nonetheless, it was a very impressive achievement, and it could hardly have been expected that any army operating from Constantinople and with such slender resources as Justinian's could have recovered Spain or Gaul, let alone more northerly provinces. Britain was left to its own devices as early as 410-11, when the Roman legions were withdrawn, and even passed into the realm of myth, so that an accomplished historian of the sixth century (Procopius) describes the province as a place whither the souls of the dead were conveyed by the classical ferryman.

Latin was still the official language in documents in Gaul, Spain,

Italy, etc, because no other written language was available. In the case of Britain, there is a darkness of nearly two centuries from the withdrawal of the legions to the landing of St Augustine of Canterbury in 597 on a mission from Pope Gregory the Great; a darkness lightened only by the fitful and very scanty documentary illumination of St Gildas. By this time, the beginnings of the seventh century, the local rulers were ceasing to behave as Roman imperial representatives and were translating their title of *Rex* much more in conformity with the kingly style to which we have for so long been accustomed. It is in these times, with the continual wearing down of the Roman civilisation, its dilution by barbaric customs and the steady growth towards nationhood of the peoples of Europe, that we find the origin of our titled system. It derives partly from a corruption of Roman titles and for the rest from the introduction of terms in the native languages. This is much more noticeable in England than in France or Spain because of the way in which the Roman civilisation was broken in Britain, as opposed to its gradual transformation in the Latin countries.

Later we shall analyse the English titular styles but for the moment a glance at them is useful as illustrating the blend of late Roman practice with Dark Age barbaric custom. The petty rulers of the Heptarchy were called kings (in Old English *cyning*, from the same root as 'kin', meaning 'race', and not as Carlyle thought, 'the cunning or skilled man'), but when one of them established a lordship over the rest he used the style of Bretwalda, or Ruler of the Britons, a curious title for an Anglo-Saxon ruler and one whose origins are lost in the past. In time, the incursions of the Northmen destroyed some of the old English kingdoms; the remainder were gathered under the aegis of Wessex, and this became the Kingdom of England. The grandson of Alfred the Great used the Greek title of Basileus, and thus England had emerged from the bickerings of the Heptarchy by a mere 150 years when the concept of empire had been grasped by her rulers.

The history of England is one of colonisation. Under the rule of the great princes of the House of Wessex, from Athelstan to Edgar the Peaceful, England colonised Celts and Northmen alike. Then came the set-back of the recrudescent Viking invasions, followed by the Norman Conquest. It is ironical that a Welsh historian, Sir Edward Lloyd, should describe the English of Edward the Confessor's time as a sluggish race who had ceased to colonise. Obviously

43

he admired virile nations, but appeared to forget that colonisation by the English, had it continued, could only have been at the expense of the Welsh. As indeed was proved 200 years later, when England had ceased to be an appanage of Norman dukes, and when once more an Edward was an English king. In 1284 Wales was conquered and incorporated with the English realm (the formal legal union came in 1542 under an English king who was half Welsh). Ireland had been nominally annexed a hundred years earlier, and Scotland remained free only by the greatest of extertions; half of France was conquered in the next century. Thus, with ebbs and flows like the tides of a mighty ocean, the sea of English colonisation has flooded many lands, until in our time the waters have receded and it now seems likely that a little England will soon be left alone, shorn even of her Welsh dependency, and of the Channel Isles and of Man.

The titles of the English kings from more than a century before the Norman Conquest were those of monarchs completely independent of an earthly superior. Hence, in the Tudor statutes which resulted from the breach with Rome, Henry VIII was reaffirming an ancient position, that the realm of England was an empire subject to no earthly power. As with so many other matters, the insularity of England caused its titled system to develop without the rigid castes of Continental noblesse.

The original English term for a nobleman was 'alderman' (*ealdorman*) which was displaced by 'earl', itself modelled on the Norse *jarl*. Alderman has survived with a very different meaning, though the attribute of seniority is usually present as it must have been in early times. After the Norman Conquest the generic terms for a nobleman was the French 'baron', but earl was never displaced and although the earl's wife is known as a countess, nothing could induce English folk to accustom themselves to a Count of Arundel or of Richmond. Duke and viscount came in due course, the former restricted at first to princes of the blood royal. Marquess was also a late importation from the Continent. Yet all ranks of the peerage below the dukes were accorded the Old English style of lord and lady. Similarly, 'knight' is not a translation of the French 'chevalier', but the Middle English form of *cnicht*, a boy or servant.

On the Continent the development of title followed far more from the relics of the Roman empire, with dukes, counts, and viscounts abounding, as the nations with their *Reges Francorum*,

Reges Hispaniorum etc, grew up to a stature which we can recognise as national. Then, in the second half of the eighth century, there occurred a great change which was to bedevil European politics for a thousand years. This turned upon the position of the Pope *vis a vis* the Frankish princes, and enormous claims in title and jurisdiction were involved. The story is an intricate mixture of hard fact, forged documents, and of legendary lore, the more powerful because it was believed to be gospel truth. 'In AD 476 Rome ceased to be the political capital of the western countries and the Papacy, inheriting no small part of the local authority which had belonged to the emperor's officers, drew to herself the reverence which the name of the city still commanded. This authority grew until, in the days which followed the Papacy's emancipation from the control of the emperors at Constantinople, the Popes had perfected in theory a scheme which made the Papacy the exact counterparts of the departed despotism, the centre of the hierarchy, the absolute mistress of the Christian world. The character of that scheme is best set forth in the singular document, most stupendous of all the medieval forgeries, which, under the name of the Donation of Constantine, commanded for seven centuries the almost unquestioning belief of mankind.' (James Bryce, *The Holy Roman Empire*, 1912, p 99.) This astonishing document was produced sometime in the eighth century. The wording can only be described as marvellous; not only is dominion over Rome, Italy and the western empire given by Constantine to Pope Sylvester (the Pope of his time), but there are precise directions as to the use by the Pope of the Lateran palace, of the diadem, the purple cloak, the sceptre, and for providing the Pope with a body of chamberlains. It must be understood that papal complicity in the production of the Donation has never been proved. In the next century another powerful concoction was produced, that of the Forged Decretals.

In all such cases there is an enormous difference between religious forgery and the work of a person seeking money or other gains for himself. From ancient times, men of deep religious faith, wishing to serve causes in which they believed, have put forth their writings under names of repute. If we are to believe the Higher Critics, this has happened with some books of the Bible, such as the Second Epistle attributed to St Peter, or the second part of the book of Isaiah. The object in using a great and revered name is to secure a better hearing, and to ensure that the teaching will be accepted; in

45

addition, the anonymous writer believes that he is really following the teaching of his source. Quite obviously this is forgery totally different from the ascriptions of feeble or indifferent work to every classical author, eg, Virgil's *Gnat*, of the *Epistles of Plato*. The authors of the Donation and the Decretals were no doubt genuinely concerned at the state of Italy, of Europe and the Church. Something should be done to right the evils. Since appeals to reason, to the existing laws, and to the Bible did not produce the desired effects, someone, probably in the papal Curia, wrote out a document which would provide the necessary weapon. One can almost hear an ecclesiastic reasoning, 'This is what should have happened, *ergo* it must have taken place.'

The forgeries reflect the state of clerical opinion in the eighth and ninth centuries. The climate of thought was itself produced by the terrible state of Italy at the time. The rule of the eastern emperor had broken down completely and the Lombards were oppressing the papal territories. The Popes appealed to the Frankish kings. Charles Martel had proved himself a warrior of heroic proportions and at the battle of Tours in 732 he had turned back the Moslem hordes which had threatened to overrun Western Europe. He was not King of the Franks, only Mayor of the Palace (somewhat reminiscent of the Great Domestic at Constantinople) to the degenerate Merovingian kings. His son, Pepin the Short, sought the aid of Pope Zacharias (741-52) and the latter soon gave a decision in Pepin's favour. The last of the *rois faineants*, Childeric III, was sent into a cloister and Pepin was anointed king in his place by St Boniface, the Englishman who was Apostle of Germany. After this, it is not surprising that King Pepin should have listened sympathetically to Pope Stephen II (752-57) when he appealed to him for aid against the Lombards. When the Pope and the King met, the latter dismounted and led the Pope's horse. In turn 'Pope Stephen anointed Pepin and his two sons, Charles and Carloman, confirming them as Kings of the Franks and creating them patricians of the Romans, and under penalty of excommunication and interdict forbidding the Franks ever to elect a king not descended from them. Thus a papal sanction consecrated the new dynasty and gave a precedent to papal claims. It may be possible that the Pope had the Byzantine emperor's authorisation to invest Pepin with the rank of patrician, but in any case the unction as such and the novel addition "of the Romans" were his own device, and implied a hereditary protectorate of Rome, not at all compatible with the emperor's sovereignty.' (*The Shorter Cambridge Medieval History*, p 301.)

In the reign of Charles the Great, Pepin's successor, an even more momentous act was performed by Pope Leo III. On Christmas Day in the year 800, Charles knelt in prayer at Mass, by the high altar of St Peter's, Rome, clad in the garments of a Roman patrician. The Gospel had been read when the Pope rose, went to Charles, placed a diadem on his brow, and then bowed before him. The Romans who filled the great church then shouted 'To Charles Augustus, crowned by God, the great and peace-giving Emperor, be life and victory.' An utterance of this kind could hardly have been spontaneous, and the whole incident must have been planned. Some there are who think that Charles was displeased and had intended to crown himself. A thousand years later Napoleon, whose sense of history was unfortunately too strong, took the crown of Lombardy and placed it on his own head while the Pope looked on.

I have often thought that there can be few worse heritages than for someone to be brought up on the legend that somewhere, at sometime, there was a title which belonged in his family and to which he is the rightful heir. I have met many such persons. Some were in moderately good financial positions, others were quite poor. All had failed to make as good a showing in life as they could have done had they used their natural abilities to full advantage. In all their work they had been continually looking back to a grandeur to which they would never attain, the thought of which vitiated all their efforts. Something of the same sort happened to medieval Europe with the coronation of Charlemagne in AD 800. This date can be taken very really as a dividing line of the middle ages; previous to 800 we have a Western Europe which is rather a poor relation of the great civilised empire based on Micklegarth, as the Viking raiders called Constantine's city. In theory, the eastern emperor is still the supreme Roman emperor; in fact, his writ does not run beyond the Balkans. The Pope has taken over most of the emperor's titles, many of his administrative powers, and now, by crowning Charlemagne, he has assumed the right—somewhat like Satan in the temptation of Christ, 'All this power will I give Thee, and the glory of them, for that is delivered unto me, and to whomsoever I will, I give it'—to bestow the kingdoms of Western Europe.

After 800, then, the Roman empire is revived in the west. The new Holy Roman Empire is not subordinate to the Roman Empire

47

at Constantinople. It is independent of earthly powers. The new
emperor is Augustus, but with this difference—a new spiritual power
has appeared in the world which can bestow crowns and dominions,
and give a just title to them. The fact that the credentials of this
power have been forged has little bearing on the developments
which will occur. The power of an idea which has been adopted as
part of the mental furniture of an age is very great, though it may
not be true or spiritually wholesome. We in the twentieth century
ought never to fail in understanding the men of the middle ages;
our own time is hag-ridden with ideas, some demonstrably false, like
the Fascist theory of master races and the Communist ideology
with its cast-iron theory of economic development; others, like the
concept of evolution, assumed by all but incapable of demonstra-
tion; and yet others, containing elements of the true and good, and
so perhaps the worst.

For a thousand years this idea of a revived Roman Empire was
to exercise its power in Europe, and, inevitably, so mighty a concept had enormous consequences in regard to titles. The papal claim
to bestow lands in Western Europe led to the invasion of Ireland
by the Anglo-Normans under Henry II (1168-72). According to
medieval ideas of feudalism, with its lords, overlords and vassals,
the Pope in bestowing the land of Ireland remained the theoretical
head of it, hence the English king was not absolute ruler of the
country, but bore the style of Lord of Ireland. Not until the reign
of Henry VIII, after the break with Rome, did he change his title
to that of King of Ireland. Then, too, in the many disputes with
the Holy See which arose in the middle ages in many countries, the
paramountcy of the Pope often prevailed. When King John of
England found himself in danger of losing his throne, he submitted
to the papal legate and agreed to hold England as a fief of the
Holy See. As this has never been retracted, it would seem that
England is still a vassal of the Vatican state. The Pope who brought
John to this humiliating position, Innocent III, obtained considerable advantages over the Kings of France, of Portugal and of Spain;
he tried, unsuccessfully, to assert his power in Norway, and his
management of the Fourth Crusade was a disaster for Christendom.
His authority was not disputed in theory.

The empire founded by the Pope for Charlemagne, despite its
legacy of troubles to Europe, did much good and was the means of
holding together a large part of central Europe. True, after Charle-

magne had divided his dominions among his sons, the new empire
was weakened for over a century, but when it eventually became
settled in one royal house its power lasted for a long time. Hobbes'
famous gibe about it was not really deserved.

Like many now defunct institutions, the Holy Roman Empire has
left deposits of title to the modern world. There are still many
persons who are counts and countesses of the Empire. The family
of the Earl of Avon possesses this title, and he could have styled
himself Count Eden. In continental Europe the parsimonious but
healthy British restriction of the status of nobility to a peer and his
wife is incomprehensible. There, all members of a noble family are
noble; hence whole trains of *noblesse*, with the inevitable concomi-
tance of a caste system.

The titles of the Emperor reflected the relative positions of
Emperor and Pope. In old pictures, when the two are shown side
by side, the papal throne is higher than the emperor's. Medieval
theologians took the words spoken at the beginning of Christ's
Passion—'Here are two swords', with His reply, 'It is enough'—to
refer to the two jurisdictions, spiritual and temporal, and as the
persons present on this occasion, the apostles, were the first bishops
of the church, the chief of them being the first Pope, the divines
of that time deduced the subordination of temporal to spiritual
jurisdiction.

To a large extent the emperors agreed to this. They were elected
persons, not military leaders or conquerors. The imperial crown was
offered to a son of Henry III of England, to Edward III (who
declined it), and to Alphonso the Wise of Castile. No position was
more strongly based in law. The emperor could be any free-born
Christian, although the empire came in time to be the prerogative
of certain families. There were for a long time seven electors—
seven having from a remote period been regarded as a mystic
number—the three archbishops of Mentz, Treves and Cologne, and
the dukes of four nations, the Franks, Swabians, Saxons and
Bavarians. Changes came during the ages, and the Palatinate of
the Rhine and the Margraviate of Brandenburg took the place of
the extinct dukedoms of Franks and Swabians. Gradually the feeling for the mystic number waned. In 1692 Emperor Leopold I gave
the House of Brunswick Luneburg an electorate, and thus it was
an elector of Hanover (which then belonged to this family) who
succeeded to the English throne in 1714 as George I.

While the eastern emperor became emperor on his succession, the western emperor was not so styled until he had been crowned. For several centuries, from the eleventh to the sixteenth, the elected emperor was styled *Romanorum rex, semper Augustus*. After being crowned at Rome, his title became *Romanorum Imperator semper Augustus*. From 1508 until the dissolution of the empire in 1806, the style was *Imperator Electus*. Maximilian I procured this privilege from the Pope, because he could not get to Rome to be crowned. The new Roman emperors bore many other titles which varied with the circumstances of the particular emperor and his period. Usually, as we shall see when examining the styles of the English kings, the monarchs of the earlier middle ages called themselves *Rex Francorum, Rex Germanorum*—of the people, that is, and not of the country. But Maximilian I used the title *Germaniae Rex*. According to Lord Bryce, the emperor Charles V had no less than seventy-five titles, though the majority of these came from his vast hereditary possessions and not from his tenure of the empire.

When the French Revolution was well under way, there was something of a mania for reviving Roman titles. Consuls and senators appeared, and Napoleon himself assumed the title of First Consul (the only one with true executive power) as a stepping-stone to his ambitions. By 1804, when he was only thirty-five, he had become Emperor of the French (not of France, be it noted). He thought seriously of remaining as Lord Paramount of Western Europe, in a kind of resuscitated feudalism, even though his career had brought something like democratic institutions to Italy and a revived nationalism to the Poles. He really did think of himself as the successor of Charlemagne, and it was probably for this reason that he brought about the demise of the Holy Roman Empire in 1806. The last of the emperors, Francis II, then took the title of Emperor of Austria, the proper dominions of his house.

Napoleon meantime proceeded with his dream of permanent empire and made an alliance with Austria by divorcing Josephine and marrying Marie Louise. The latter bore him the son he had so ardently desired in order to perpetuate his dynasty. This son he named King of Rome, in direct imitation of the custom, gradually developed under the empire, by which the emperor's eldest son was known as *Rex Romanorum*. Napoleon's empire fell to pieces, of course, after his defeat at Waterloo, but it left its legacy to France and through France to the world. One of Napoleon's nephews succeeded in following him, becoming democratic chief of France as her president, and then, by a skilful *coup de main*, made himself Emperor of the French. His title was that of Napoleon III. Who, then, was the Second Napoleon? The King of Rome, or Duke de Reichstadt, who died young. Napoleon III brought back to the French the imperial idea; the Second Empire was a time of great but brittle brilliance and ended in the terrible defeats of 1870-71, when the French emperor was lucky to find refuge in England. The end of Bonapartism as a dynastic force came with the death of the Prince Imperial, son of Napoleon III, while serving as a volunteer with the British Army in Zululand in 1876. But the delusion of Napoleonic grandeur has not yet been exorcised from the French mind, as anyone could discern in the less responsible utterances of the former French president, General de Gaulle. It exposes France to the danger of striving after a greatness which no longer exists.

In the sphere of title, France's many changes of regime since 1789 have produced a variety of peers graded according to the political circumstances which gave them birth, in contrast to the peculiar English titled system which is at least a natural growth.

The title of emperor has been bestowed far more widely in modern than in ancient times. To the Romans of the undivided dominion up to the age of Diocletian, there could be only one emperor. Diocletian's experiment with two Augusti and two Caesars did not last long. Nor was the restoration of a single rulership under Constantine of Theodosius the Great of longer endurance. With the latter's death in 395, the eastern and western parts of the empire came under separate rule. Then, from 800 onwards, there is one sole and now 'Holy' Roman emperor again; the existence of the true successor of Augustus and Constantine in the east being disregarded, probably on the ground that he was a schismatic. In the year 1054 occurred that breach between the eastern and western churches which has produced the Orthodox church and the Roman Catholic church of today (happily the anathemas pronounced on both sides have now been withdrawn, and the possibilities of reunion are being tentatively discussed). Certainly in Dante's carefully reasoned treatise, *De Monarchia*, written about 1312, only one empire and one emperor are envisaged throughout by the author. Nor did this position alter for five centuries after Dante. Napoleon's short-lived empire was contemporary not only with the Austrian empire but also with the Russian. Further away, the rulers of China and Japan

51

were called emperors by the Europeans; so, too, was the Great Mogul of India, and possibly the Shah of Persia. A sudden cultus of the imperial title arose in the nineteenth century. Brazil became an empire ruled by a member of the House of Braganza; so, too, for a very short time did Mexico under the unfortunate Maximilian of Austria, abandoned to a firing squad by Napoleon III. Even Haiti had its Emperor Jones! (Incidentally, there is a beautifully produced work of some size on the Orders of Chivalry of Haiti.)

Then, in 1877, the title of the British sovereign joined the now fashionable collection, when Queen Victoria became Empress of India. In 1871 the German emperor had been proclaimed. The 1914-18 war finished three empires—Russia, Austria and Germany. The British Empire was unable to survive its own victory in 1945. For some six years the King of Italy enjoyed the title of Emperor of Ethiopia. Today, the only persons still on their thrones and referred to as emperors are the hereditary sovereigns of Ethiopia and Japan; and for both of them the title of emperor is a western description. Apart from these instances, the title of emperor and the concept of empire have both completely disappeared. This is not to say that the power vacuum left by the dissolved empires of the Europeans has not been filled by other rulers.

NOTE: The Ironies of History. The last emperor of the western Roman empire was named Romulus Augustulus, the former being the name of Rome's founder, and the latter a diminutive of the name of Rome's first emperor. The last emperor of the eastern, or Byzantine, empire, who was killed in 1453, was Constantine XI, bearing the same name as the founder of Constantinople, Constantine the Great, who made the city named after himself the capital of the eastern Roman empire.

At the end of the Prophecy of St Malachy, concerning the succession of the Popes, there is this remarkable passage: *In persecutione extrema Sacrae Romanae Ecclesiae sedebit Petrus Romanus qui pascet oves in multis tribulationibus, quibus transactis, civitas septicollis diruetur, et Judex tremendus judicabit populum*: 'During the last persecution of the Holy Roman Church there shall sit Peter the Roman who shall feed his flock among great tribulations and, these being passed, the city of the seven hills shall be utterly destroyed and the awful Judge will judge the people.' (Herbert Thurston, S.J., *The War and the Prophets*, 1915, p 159.) The identity of name between the first (or greatest) monarch of a line and the last is further illustrated in the history of the ancient empires of America. Montezuma II, the last but one Aztec sovereign of Mexico, bore the name of the ruler who, in the middle of the fifteenth century, had expanded Aztec dominion to the shores of the Gulf of Mexico. In the other great American empire, that of Peru, Manco, the last of the Incas, bore the name of the founder, Manco Capac.

52

6. The Rise of Islam

While the emperors of Constantinople vainly endeavoured to retain even a shadowy authority over their erstwhile western provinces, some of the most valuable portions of their empire in the east were wrested from their grasp by a sudden movement in one of the least known and most neglected parts of the globe. The story goes that when Alexander the Great had returned to Babylon after his successful invasion of India, no envoys came from Arabia to join the throng of ambassadors who paid court to the new Great King. When Alexander realised that the Arabs were taking no notice of him, he prepared an expedition by sea and land to bring these insolent people to submission. He died before he could set out on this fresh career of conquest, and the Arabs were left in their solitude for another thousand years.

To the emperor Heraclius (reigned 610-41) the most pressing political problem was to know how to cope with the increasing power of Persia. From Constantinople, he had seen the bivouac fires of the Persian host encamped on the Asian shores of his dominions. One after another of his provincial capitals had fallen to the Persians, who had even captured the True Cross at Jerusalem. Then, at last, the tide turned in Heraclius' favour; he decisively defeated the Persians, regained the Cross (found by St Helena, mother of Constantine the Great), and re-established his dominions. While he rested on his victories, he suddenly received an embassy, if such it could be called, from some rough-looking denizens of the Arabian peninsula. They presented to the emperor a terse message calling on him to submit to one Mohammed, who called himself the Prophet of God. The emperor's contemptuous indignation may be imagined, though it might have been some consolation for what he must have regarded as an insult had he known that the Persian king had also received a similar message.

The world was to be transformed as a result of these messages. In

53

the particular matter of our study of titles, a whole series of new terms was to enter the lingua franca of the nations, and to understand how this came about one must know something of the meaning of Islam. This word means 'to submit to God'. Predestination is as much a tenet of Islam as it is of historical Calvinism. In passing, it should be noted that believers in Islam do not refer to themselves as Mohammedans. They are followers of Mohammed but they do not worship him, and they regard Christians as having fallen into grave error in believing in the deity of Christ.

There are few phenomena in history more impressive than the rise and rapid diffusion of Islam. The story has frequently been told, but its wonder never ceases. A poor, almost illiterate Arabian youth, subject to epilepsy, becomes camel-driver and steward to a rich widow, whom he marries and with whom he settles down to a life of happiness and respectability in his native town of Mecca. At the age of forty he begins to see visions, hear voices, and feel impelled to preach a new religion to his idolatrous countrymen. Obstructed, derided at every turn, with his life at times in danger, he at last receives a call to another town, Medina, where a favourable hearing is vouchsafed him. Marshalling the Medinese forces, he at length becomes too strong for the Meccans, who bow to him whom they formerly rejected. Entering Mecca in triumph, he abolishes idolatry, establishes a pure monotheism, and converts the tribes of Arabia to this faith in the one God and in himself as the Prophet of God. At the age of sixty-three in the year AD 632 (11 of the Hegira, or Flight to Medina, from which the Islamic era dates), he dies peacefully and is succeeded in authority by his closest friend, Abu Bekr. Such is a merest outline of the life of Mohammed. Within a century of his death, the Islamic world extends from the Atlantic shores into India, from Spain to Egypt. The religion is without priest, or church; it is spread by laymen for laymen, and no barriers of race or colour are recognised. Those who accept Islam, who surrender to God, are the true believers. The rest are infidels. To this day, although several lands which were overrun by the Moslems have been reclaimed for Christianity and European civilisation, as in Spain and the Balkans, the fact remains that the once mighty African church in North Africa has disappeared, while in Egypt and the Middle East, Christianity, although it survives, is the faith of a downtrodden minority. So great an influence on the world could not fail to give rise to new titles.

A vast literature exists on the history of the Caliphate. The title Caliph means 'successor', ie, to the Prophet Mohammed—hence Caliph Rasul Allah, Successor of the Prophet of God—and the history of the Caliphate is extremely chequered. It provides a parallel to the story of the Holy Roman Empire, but with marked differences. When the theory behind the revival of the Roman Empire in the person of Charlemagne caught the imagination of Western Europe, there was, as mentioned in the last chapter, the twofold conception of the emperor as ruler of the world, with the Pope beside him, possessing the spiritual functions and authority of the Vicar of Christ. To the early church, the Roman empire and civilisation had appeared to be almost co-terminous. From, at latest, the sixth century, the authority of the eastern emperor became more and more nominal, and this, combined with disagreements between the eastern church and the western church headed by the Pope, made it natural for the Popes to turn elsewhere for temporal help. They turned, as we have seen, to the Frankish kings, culminating in the alleged revival of Roman imperial authority in the west in the person of Charlemagne and his successors.

But though there are parallels in the histories of the Caliphate and the Holy Roman Empire, in origins the former is completely different from the latter. The Caliphate had no theory behind it, but arose out of the death of Mohammed and the need to find someone to continue his teachings. When it had become an office, the Moslem theologians found support for the institution in the Koran, or if not there, then in the Hadith, or Traditions, which were held to be derived from the Prophet.

A fundamental difference between Islam and Christianity is that in the former there is nothing resembling the Papacy. The Caliph, however, exalted in power, remains a layman. Anyone can read the prayers in the mosque. From time to time, in European writing about Islam, one sees references to Moslem priests, but no such persons exist. There are 'imans' in many mosques but they are, as their title implies, only leaders.

The first Caliph, Abu Bekr, was elected by the principal Moslems on the day of Mohammed's death. He lived for two years and was succeeded by Omar who, after a successful Caliphate of ten years, was killed by an assassin. Before he died he is considered by Moslem theologians to have nominated several electors who were to choose the next Caliph. Whether this is or is not correct, there was an element of election in the case of the first four Caliphs, and this persisted right up to the time of the Turkish Caliphs, or Sultans of Turkey. We are reminded of the fact that the English monarchy was once elective and that this theory is enshrined as part of the coronation service of every British sovereign.

The third Caliph, Othman, was killed by rebel Moslems in AD 656. The fourth Caliph, Aly, the Prophet's son-in-law, was then elected, but died in 661 as the result of an assassin's attack. Islam should have been free of the dissensions, heresies and schisms which must necessarily attend an elaborate system of dogma but, as in all other human communities of belief, there are, in fact, bitter sectarian differences among Moslems. There are those who think that the first three Caliphs were usurpers and that Aly was the rightful successor to the Prophet. They are known as Shiites, or sectaries. The majority of Moslems adhere to the orthodox position and accept the first three Caliphs as Mohammed's legitimate successors.

Quite apart from this schism in Islam, many other dissensions arose over the office of Caliph. Aly was not sole Caliph. Muavia held a large part of the Moslem world and after Aly's death became sole Caliph. He was the founder of the Omayyad dynasty and established his throne at Damascus. However, in the year 750 the Omayyads were defeated and leadership of the Moslems passed to the Abbasids, the descendants of Abbas, the uncle of Mohammed. A member of the Omayyad family escaped from the ruin of their fortunes and reached Spain, where he set up an independent kingdom. The glory of the Abbasids was short-lived. After a lingering and humiliating Caliphate in Baghdad as virtual prisoners of their own soldiers, the end came in 1258 when the savage hordes of the Mongols captured Baghdad and put the Caliph to death. A survivor of this disaster was invited to Egypt and there installed with great pomp as Caliph, but with no real power. The shadow of a shadowy authority, it endured for two and a half centuries, during which the Caliphs were used by the Sultans of Egypt to give legality to their position while Moslem princes applied to them from time to time for *de jure* recognition of their *de facto* possession of power.

The last of the Caliphs in Egypt was taken prisoner when the Mameluke Sultans of that country were overthrown by the Osmanli Turks. Mutawakhil, the last Caliph, resigned his title to the Turkish Sultan, Selim. As the principal Moslem sovereign, the Sultan of

Turkey was styled Caliph until the end of the Turkish empire. The last of the line was exiled from Turkey in 1924. The country had become a republic in 1922, and in 1924 the Caliphate was abolished, one of the many monarchical casualties of the first world war. The sultanate of Turkey was succeeded by a republic, of which the first president was Kemal Ataturk. The changes in the president's name and style followed upon his growing repute with his countrymen. Born as Mustafa, he received the *cognomen* of Kemal (meaning 'perfection'), from a schoolmaster who was impressed by his ability. After the Turkish War of Independence, 1919-22, he was known as Mustafa Kemal Pasha (ie, chief); then the national assembly bestowed on him the title of Ghazi (anti-infidel or veteran warrior). As Ghazi Pasha he was known until 1934 when, by his own decision, adoption of surnames became compulsory. He then took the name of Ataturk ('Father Turk').

So much for the history, in brief, of this institution. During the bulk of its existence, the Caliphate had a strong resemblance to the Merovingian monarchy in France, when the degenerate descendants of Clovis—*les rois fainéants*—were paraded on ceremonial occasions until the real rulers, the mayors of the Palace, assumed these titles as well as the realities of power. (Another comparison is with the Mogul emperors of India, who also called themselves Caliphs, and whose nominal authority at Delhi endured until after the Indian Mutiny.)

Despite the harsh reality of the Caliphate, the theory blossomed out in a manner worthy of medieval Europe. To the speculative theologians and jurists of Islam, the Caliph continued, ideally at least, as head of the Moslem world, while pious Moslems of the holy cities of Mecca and Medina saw in the Omayyad dynasty the transformation of the Caliphate into a temporal sovereignty.

Other titles were later given to the holder of the office of Caliph and the second Caliph, Omar, at first bore the style, Caliph of the Caliph of the Apostle of God. This, being somewhat awkward, was altered to the simpler Caliph, used once only. Omar also assumed the title of Amir ul Mu'Minim, or Commander of the Faithful, a style familiar to many westerners through its use in works such as the Arabian Nights. In the middle ages this was rendered under forms such as 'elmiram mommini' and 'miralomin', these perverted versions of the Caliph's title and similarly distorted accounts of the Moslem faith being typical of medieval Europe's vast ignorance of the facts about the Islamic religion. In one contemporary Christian account of the First Crusade, a Moslem leader is actually made to swear by his gods!

The early Caliphs could be described by one of these titles: Caliph, Amir ul Mu'Minim, and Imam. The last term means 'leader, guide or model', and describes the man who leads the prayers in the mosque. When used as a title of the Caliph, it refers to his religious activity as head of the state. The term 'Amir' etc, denotes his authority as the supreme ruler in war and in peace. In order to support the theory of the Caliphate, the Moslem theologians, like their Christian counterparts, have sought justification in texts from the Koran. The word 'Caliphah' is used in several passages in the Koran to denote 'successors' as applied to the true believers (the Moslems), but in two passages referring to Adam and to David the implication is that these were vicegerents of God. These two texts were held to justify the institution of the Caliphate, much as the two swords mentioned in St Luke's Gospel (ch 22, v 38) figure forth the two powers—Pope and Emperor—of spiritual and temporal sovereignty. In the Traditions of Islam (Hadith) there is a clear rule that the Caliph must belong to the Koreish, the Meccan tribe of which Mohammed was a member. 'This qualification was fulfilled throughout the whole of the historical period proper—in the persons of the Ommayad and Abbasid Caliphs, as it was also in the case of their Shiah rivals, the Fatimids of Egypt.' (Sir Thomas Arnold, *The Caliphate*, 1924, p 47.)

Such, then, is this celebrated title which once belonged to the most powerful monarch in the world, but which, in course of centuries, came to be adopted by Moslem rulers in quite small states. The world of the Caliphs was so different from that of today that there is no longer any place even in Moslem regions for such a supreme ruler.

As the term 'Koran' has been used more than once above, it is as well to be quite clear as to its meaning; literally it denotes 'reading' or 'recitation'. The Koran is, of course, the sacred book or bible of of Islam, which Moslems believe to contain the revelation God made to Mohammed, most of it written down after the Prophet's death. In this respect it resembles the New Testament which was written after the earthly lifetime of Christ. Another interesting parallel with Christianity is the existence of the Hadith, or Traditions, in Islam, which date from some centuries later than the Koran. Just as it is impossible to find every practice of the church in the New Testament, so Moslem theologians have had two sources of revelation, as in the Catholic Church. Scripture and apostolic traditions correspond very roughly to Koran and Hadith.

Other terms of interest in connection with Islam are 'Sultan', meaning Power or Ruler, *Minbar* meaning Pulpit (in the mosque), and *Ulama*, ie, the Learned. The last term is almost the equivalent of the *jurisconsulti* of ancient Rome, those learned lawyers whose opinions had nearly the force of law. The Koran resembles in its contents more the Old Testament than the New, though it does include a striking testimony to the Virgin Birth of Christ (to the confusion of Modernist or *avant garde* Christian theologians). It has a much more legalistic flavour than the testaments, and consequently the *Ulama* are more akin to legal than to theological experts. Owing to the Unitarian theory of monotheism advanced by Mohammed, there is no speculation in Islam as to the nature of God similar to the Trinitarian controversies among Christians; and of course the long-drawn-out contests in the church on Christology are unmatched in Moslem internal strife. Mohammed taught that there had been many prophets, Abraham, Moses and Christ being among them. Although Christ was born of the Virgin, the Lady Miriam (Mary), He was only human. He was not crucified, only caught up by God and saved from death. The Mahdi, the opponent of General Gordon in the Sudan, expected that Christ would descend from heaven to meet him when his conquests had reached Jerusalem.

The term 'Sultan' has been widely used over many centuries. It has applied to rulers of empires like the Sultan of Turkey and to petty princelings in the Dutch East Indies. Sultana, applied to the mother, wife or daughter of a sultan, appears to be an Italianate formation from the masculine term.

The Mahdi is one who is guided aright. In the history of Islam there have been many movements designed to foster a return to the purity of the pristine faith, among them those led by the Wahhabis, or Puritans of Islam. The story of the Mahdi who, in the second half of the nineteenth century, appeared in the Sudan, tore it from the Egyptians and was responsible for the death of Gordon, is well known. Islam is more liable than any other faith to the sudden appearance of such enthusiasts, for at its base is the practice known as the *jihad*, or holy war. This should be waged against the infidels by the true believers, and although the realities of political life have forced toleration of non-Moslems upon Moslem states, there is always the undercurrent of desire to propagate the faith by force of arms. The half-mad, half-mystic fanatic can soon put a torch to the gunpowder of Islamic bigotry, and his followers will charge into machine-gun fire, certain that death for the faith will bring the rewards of paradise, the ministrations of the houris beside the still waters. Such was the inspiration of the Mad Mullah ('mullah' being another name given to the learned in Islam) of Somaliland after the first world war; such was the strength of the opposition to King Amanullah of Afghanistan in the late 1920s when he sought to modernize his kingdom.

The term 'Amir', used by the second Caliph, Omar, is second only to that of 'Sultan' in its widespread application to Moslem rulers. The Amir, or Ameer, of Afghanistan is the title of the king of that country. The Emirs (a form of Amir) are Moslem rulers, sometimes only over tribes in parts of Africa and western Asia, hence the term 'emirate', familiar to us from its use in Nigeria.

Although the Moslems did not remain united politically for more than a very few generations, Moslem powers remained a terror to Christian Europe for a thousand years. Every child who has read the romances of Guy of Warwick, or of King Horn, knows that the Saracens are ubiquitous, always malevolent and destructive, and usually present in great numbers. Against them the Christian hero has ever to fight with desperate courage. These romances reflect a background of historical fact. Throughout medieval Christendom all knew of the existence of a mighty paynim power, that of the Saracens and later of the Turks. Checked in France in 732, the Islamic flood fell back behind the Pyrenees, but 700 years were to pass before Spain became Christian again. The islands of the Mediterranean were occupied by the Saracens and had to be reconquered. Rome itself was sacked by them. Europe's counter-attack in the Crusades wrested the Holy Land from the Moslems but the Christians failed to retain it. The wicked Fourth Crusade, while doing no harm to the Moslems, fatally weakened the eastern empire, and with the rise of the Turkish power the capture of Constantinople became a certainty. Western Europe sent no aid, and the city fell to the Sultan Mohammed II in 1453. Soon, the whole of the Balkans came under Turkish domination or the threat of it. Bulgaria was ruled by the Turks from 1398 to 1878; Servia from 1459 to 1804, and was not finally freed until 1878; Montenegro was not clear of them until the nineteenth century, and Greece suffered them for 400 years. Moreover the Turks pressed on with invasions of Austria and on more than one occasion seriously threatened Vienna.

Is it any wonder that the Europeans should have given to the Sultan titles expressive of the great impression he made upon them? The Great or Grand Soldan is the title under which he is mentioned quite soberly in European writings of medieval times. He is accorded great respect, rather on the principle of letting 'the devil be sometime honoured for his burning throne'. In the medieval rolls of arms there is often included the armorial achievement of the Grand Soldan; heraldry is almost exclusively a western European invention but the principal oriental personages were assumed by virtue of their very greatness to bear these insignia of honour.

In more modern periods the Sultan becomes the Great or Grand Turk. To Europeans he appears in the guise that the King of Persia wore to the Greeks, as the King or the Great King. Other forms of description are the Grand Seignior (ie, French *Seigneur*; Latin *senior*). This French usage is in keeping with the references to their own royal great ones as Monsieur, Madame or Mademoiselle, eg, the *Grande Mademoiselle*, who was always going to marry distinguished men in Louis XIV's earlier reign, or *le Grand Batarde* of Burgundy (to an Englishman it is irresistibly amusing for anyone in court circles to be styled the French equivalent of Big Bastard!).

The Grand Seignior was a good term to use of an absolute monarch, whose power knew no check save that of assassination in a conspiracy. The name 'Sublime Porte' or 'Ottoman Porte' was often used of the Sultan, as though he summed up, or collectivised, his nation. In fact, La Sublime Porte, or High Gate, was the Turkish description of the central office of their administration. As the latter was a despotism, the term was not inapt when used of the sultan. The adjective 'Ottoman' referred to the descent of the dynasty from Othman, or Osman I, and was applied to the whole race, as in Ottoman Turks, or simply Ottomans.

It is impossible not to sense a certain admiration behind the terms in which, during the centuries of Turkish power, Europeans referred to the Sultan, though in truth, unless one accords the adjective 'sublime' or 'grand' to successful wickedness, the Turks and their sovereigns deserve no admiration whatever. By the eighteenth century, their power to molest Europe had been checked and, in the nineteenth century their ability to degrade Hellas gradually declined. Their record is one of cruelty, oppression and misrule. Yet when Turkey had become the Sick Man of Europe there was no lack of British statesmen to bolster up the ramshackle Ottoman empire. The Crimean War was fought to this end, and the Treaty of Berlin in 1878, the famous 'peace with honour' of Disraeli, aimed at preserving the *status quo*. Right up to the 1914-18 war, Britain was worried over the designs of Russia, particularly of the possibility of an advance through Central Asia against India. Readers of *The Martyrdom of Man* by Winwood Reade will recall how strangely this doubting Victorian, with his extremely radical views on religion, could yet accept blindly the political ideas of his time. He forecasts battles between disciplined Asiatics led by Russian and British officers to decide the future of Asia. The magazines of the early part of this century contain many stories in which Britain and Russia are at grips in Asia. Mouldering now in disused corners of libraries in military clubs are books, once thought alarmist and daring, telling how Russia's aims in Asia should be countered. In the eyes of our statesmen, Constantinople, as the key to the straits between Europe and Asia, was of no danger so long as it remained in Turkish hands. At all costs it must be kept from becoming a Russian possession. Yet at last, when the war with Germany made Russia our ally and Turkey our enemy, we had perforce to alter our policy. When Britain and her allies had won the war, Constantinople was to go to Russia, and to help accomplish this the British tried to force the Dardanelles, an exploit which could have changed the course of modern history. Had it succeeded, there would have been no collapse of Russia, no Bolshevik revolution, and quite possibly a negotiated peace with a still Hohenzollern Germany. As things turned out, by a most strange twist of history, the aims of the Victorian statesmen were accomplished and the straits remained in Turkish hands.

The Ottoman or Turkish empire in its heyday was of much the same extent as the Byzantine empire under Justinian. With such wide dominions, it was inevitable that considerable use should be made of the system of viceroys, and one of the most important of these was the Khedive of Egypt. The Turks conquered Egypt in 1517, and the country was ruled by Turkish pashas, a term used by the Turks to describe a person who held a high administrative position either in civil or military affairs. Pashas were said to be pashas of one, two or three tails, according to the

62

symbol of a horse's tail which they used in war. Bashaw is another form of the word, perhaps closer to the Turkish original which means a chief (as with Ataturk in his earlier days). In 1805, after the confusion caused in Egypt by Napoleon's invasion in 1798 and subsequent withdrawal, an Albanian of high military rank, Mehemet Ali, became Pasha, or Governor, of Egypt by popular acclaim. He was confirmed in this position by the Sultan of Turkey but then endeavoured to become an independent ruler. His armies over-ran the Near East but he was eventually forced to remain content with Egypt and the Sudan, his status being that of a vali, or viceroy with the right of hereditary government of Egypt under the Sultan. In 1867 his grandson, Ismail, obtained the Sultan's permission to style himself the Khedive, a word meaning 'master' or 'prince'. He remained technically the Sultan's viceroy, though in most respects he was independent. The office was known as the Khedivate, and the chief wife's title was that of Khediva.

In 1882 a strange situation arose. Owing to the Khedive's mismanagement of his financies, the British occupied Egypt, thus taking over part of what still remained officially the Sultan's empire. They remained in control until 1914, when the fact that they were at war with Turkey made it imperative for them to terminate the novel constitutional position of Egypt. A British protectorate over the country was proclaimed on 18 December 1914, the Khedive was deposed, and his uncle put in to succeed him with the title of Sultan. In 1922, after much national agitation, the British decided to end the protectorate and to set up an independent kingdom, but with certain matters still remaining under British control. The Egyptian kings were Fuad (1922-36), Farouk (1936-52) and, for a very short while, Farouk's infant son. The monarchy was succeded by a republic which, along with the royal office, abolished the old titles such as that of pasha.

During the British occupation of Egypt the command of the Egyptian army was held by a British subject, and his title was that of Sirdar, a term derived from an Urdu and Persian word meaning 'head' and 'holding', thus denoting a leader, or person in command.

Before leaving Egypt for other parts of the former Ottoman empire, mention should be made of the Janissaries and the Mamelukes, as these words partake of the nature of titles. The Janissaries, a term meaning 'new soldiers,' were instituted in 1330 and at first were composed of Christians forced to become Moslems, or of the children of Christians who were educated as Moslems. They were picked troops, allowed many privileges but bound to celibacy. At the capture of Constantinople they were foremost in the storming of the walls. Detachments of them were stationed throughout the empire. The Janissary corps was a hotbed of intrigue and was at last abolished by the Sultan of Turkey in 1826, though in so doing he had to burn some 8,000 of them in their barracks and execute another 15,000.

The Mamelukes, or Manluks, were also a force recruited from the Christians or Circassians, and the term means 'a purchased slave'. They seized control in Egypt in 1249 and remained very much the rulers under their sultans and beys until their power was broken by Napoleon's army.

Everyone who has visited Egypt must know the title of 'effendi' given as a mark of respect. At first, it was used by the Turks for their government officials and members of learned professions, and hence applied to many foreigners, especially if they were likely to produce a gratuity. It is said to derive from a Greek word.

The sprawling awkward outrage of an Ottoman empire produced yet more titles. One was that of 'Bey', which meant simply 'a governor', the district over which he ruled being known as his 'bey-lic.' Bey is a Turkish word and was formerly spelt 'beg'. The most famous of beys is the Bey of Tunis, whose history extends from the eighteenth to the present century. In 1957 the office of Bey was abolished and Tunisia became a republic. Previously, the Bey's duties included the management of the tribes in Tunisia and the collection of taxes. The Turks had reconquered Tunis from the Spaniards in 1574, and a pasha was appointed in charge of the government of the country. In a short time there was a revolution among the troops, the famous Janissaries, who elected a Dey with supreme power. The term 'Dey' means literally, a maternal uncle, and was a title often given to the head of the local Janissaries. Here, too, is a title of office which became hereditary in the family of the Dey of Algiers. To return to the Deys of Tunis, their government lasted until 1705 but their importance was undermined by the growth of power in the Beys, an office which had become hereditary from 1631 to 1702 in the family of a Corsican renegade, Murad. The house of Murad was wiped out by the last Dey, Ibrahim, whose reign lasted from 1702 to 1705, and who was killed in battle with

64

the Algerians. Then Hussein ben'Ali, the son of another (Cretan) renegade, was elected sovereign, ie, Bey, by the Janissaries. Under his rule the title and position became hereditary in his family, which survived until the end, when the final Bey was Sid Mohammed Lamine Pasha. He was treated with punctilious ceremony by the French during their government of Tunisia because they felt they needed him to bolster up their own position. In the person of the Bey of Tunis we meet the first example in this book of what can only be adequately described as 'second league' or 'third class' monarchy. The Bey was regarded by his French masters as technically a sovereign, yet he was not a king, and his style was that of Highness, but not Majesty. He was called in French, *Possesseur du Royaume de Tunis, Souverain Actuel.* The hereditary element in the Bey's status was very strange, because succession passed to the oldest member of the Beylical family. The heir to the throne was called by the French, the *Bey du Camp*, and the Bey's wife was the Beza.

Moving westward along the North African coast, we come to Algeria where a type of government existed from 1659 to 1830 under the name of the Deys of Algiers. Probably no part of the Turkish dominions was ever so badly managed as was the truly anarchial Algeria. The capital city was a nest of pirates and though it was several times bombarded by European fleets, it did not cease to be a curse to the peoples of the Mediterranean until 1830, when, the last of the Deys having insulted the French consul by flicking him with a fly whisk, the French landed in force and in time took over the whole country. During the French conquest their most determined opponent was Abd-el-Kader, who had been a marabout, or Moslem hermit. 'Marabout' is also the name given to the burial place or shrine of a Moslem saint—little edifices which are seen everywhere in Algeria—so that the term is thus associated not only with dead holy men but also with the living who are regarded as saints.

The rise and progress of Islam have created a whole world of titles, and this does not include oriental titles as such, since Islam is really allied to the West. The religion is akin to Judaism and to Christianity; it is theistic whereas the religions of India and the Far East are not. In any account of the 'wisdom of the West' place must be found for Arabic influence, because it is to the western world that Islam really pertains. Before passing, therefore, to consider

E

the titled systems of India and China, we must pay attention to the evolution of monarchial titles in Western Europe.

NOTE: Mufti. This is another term for those learned in the law in Islam. Their position corresponds perhaps most closely to that of canonists in the Latin church. The opinions of the mufti are given to the cadi, or judge, who then can apply them to the case in point. The word 'mufti' is Arabic, and by a strange application the word has become synonymous in English with the wearing of civilian clothes by those who are in the military service. In this connection it is said to be of Anglo-Indian origin, and may, it is suggested, have been derived from the flowing robes worn by muftis. Before the changes in Turkey, there was a Chief, or Grand Mufti in that country who was responsible for religious affairs, as the Grand Vizier was for political matters. The vizir, or vizier, has now become purely a figure of historical or romantic association; the word is said to be Arabic and to mean 'a porter', or one who carries burdens, hence its application to the chief minister of the sultan.

7. Titles in Western Europe

The Holy Roman Empire constituted such an important factor in the politics of Western Europe that it is relevant to ask, how far did its jurisdiction extend? Was England even regarded as part of the Empire? Did Charlemange treat with Offa, King of Mercia, as an equal, or did he look upon him as in some sort a vassal? We have seen that from very early times, indeed from the Heptarchy, the English kings regarded themselves and their realm as free from the control of other powers (with the possible exception of John's fealty to the Papacy!). In the preambles of one of his Acts of Parliament, Henry VIII was therefore merely reaffirming a position taken up for some 900 years. It has been suggested that the visit of the Emperor Sigismund to Henry V to try to mediate over the war with France was the interference of a feudal superior. If so, the view must have been held by Sigismund only. It was definitely repudiated in England. In any event there was freedom from outside control in any matter of title in England, with important consequences.

In Continental lands, however, the Empire's impingement upon matters of title was very real and the history even of regal titles was largely conditioned by the extent to which their owners owed allegiance to the Empire. Denmark, for example, owed fealty to the Emperor for some time prior to the death of Frederick II.

Some earlier authorities in the middle ages thought that the College of Electors, which chose the Emperor, was composed of six members; whereas, generally the mystic number of seven prevailed. The title of Elector came, however, to rank in importance almost immediately after that of king, and in due time, an eighth and finally a ninth Elector was added to the College. Napoleon in his role of Grand Feudatory began to arrange the ancient kingdoms and principalities as Charlemagne had not done. He gave the title of Elector to the Duke of Wurtemberg, the Margrave of Baden, the Landgrave of Hesse-Cassel, and the Archbishop of Salzburg. This was in 1803, three years before he brought the whole system to an end.

Very early in medieval Europe we have the emergence of the Counts Palatine, especially familiar to English readers because the Count Palatine, or Palsgrave, was the son-in-law of James I of England. The word 'Palatine' comes from *Palatium*, or Palace, and thus denotes someone who has a special relationship with a king's or emperor's palace. The Counts Palatine generally mentioned in history are those of the Rhineland and the areas from which they took their titles were usually debatable lands on a frontier. The ruler of a county palatine is virtually a viceroy wielding the powers of a sovereign and though, for the obvious reason of size, there was little chance of this type of feudal jurisdiction developing in England, we do nonetheless come upon districts in England which were known as Palatinates. One, the earldom of Chester, given by William the Conqueror to Hugh Lupus, was regarded as particularly important owing to its proximity to North Wales. The title has long been annexed to that of the Prince of Wales, so that when the sovereign's eldest son is thus created, he also thereby becomes Earl of Chester.

In another instance, that of Durham, the peculiar jurisdiction of the palatinate was given to the bishops of the see, and the Bishop of Durham was said anciently to have *omnia jura regalia et omnes libertates regales infra libertatem suam Dunelmensem*. 'All the royal rights and liberties within his liberty of Durham.' At the time of the Norman Conquest this special jurisdiction was thought to be necessary because of the proximity and ill-defined nature of the Scottish border. Not until the time of William II was Cumberland properly to be reckoned as English. The status of the Bishops of Durham resembled that of the Prince Bishops (eg, of Liege) on the Continent where the prelate was a temporal as well as a spiritual ruler. At some times, too, the earldom of Pembroke was called a palatinate, and this title was perhaps used last of the Duchy of Lancaster, which remains annexed to the Crown.

A title mentioned among the Electors of the Empire was that of Margrave. This is really the equivalent of the English marquess (often spelt 'marquis' in popular accounts), or perhaps it would be better to say that it is the original of our marquessate. It means the ruler or keeper of a mark or limit, ie, of the empire. The German, *mark*, a border, and *graf*, a count, gives Margrave, whence the

68

feminine Margravate, or Margraviate, to denote the thing itself, while the lady is termed Margravine. In Latin, the word is *marchio* or *margravius*. In Dutch it is *marckgrave*, and in Italian, *marchese*. The title, clearly Germanic, occurs first in the dispositions of Charlemagne, and has since become native to all the languages of Europe. In England, there were no marquesses until the fifteenth century, but the word 'march', as denoting a frontier, was used long before that time. Its particular application in this country was to the frontier between England and Wales, and if ever an area deserved the title of 'wild west' it was this district, exposed to the incursions of the Welsh on one side and the reprisals of the English Marcher Lords on the other. These nobles were a nexus of influential families who came to exercise great power, quite apart from their function in maintaining control over the frontier. None of them bore the title of marquess; they were barons and earls. By a curiosity, the title entered the English peerage when a Welsh frontier had ceased to be a problem. No English marquess was ever a hard-hitting, hard-riding western marshal.

Before going on to the royal titles of England, Spain, France, Portugal, all countries outside the Empire, some of the lesser states of Europe are of interest in that their rulers used (in the case of Monaco, still use) the title of Serene Highness. Some old writers refer to princes who, not being entirely sovereign or entirely independent, did not use the term Majesty but were known as Highness or *Serenitas*. Such princes were the Dukes of Saxony, of Bavaria, of Lombardy, of Florence etc. Protocol and precedence were of great importance to the rulers of Europe, just as they are in the United Nations Assembly now. The use of the term Serene Highness was, therefore, a very diplomatic way of smoothing ruffled feelings, and in this sense we can understand why Serene as applied to various German princes is considered a translation of *durchlaucht* serene.

An outstanding case was that of the Doge of Venice. He was known as the Most Serene *(Serenissimus)*. Venice could not fairly be described as a dependency, even in its infancy, of any country; the older account of its having been formed by fugitives who fled to the swamps to escape Attila and his Huns, has, it seems, to be treated with reserve; the lagoons already possessed inhabitants. Whatever its commencement, the Venetian state owed nothing to any other and as it grew to greatness many others owed much to

69

it. Venice was one of the great banking centres of Europe, and the carrier trade with the Levant was in its hands, as the Crusaders discovered, and the Greeks to their cost in the Fourth Crusade. The Doge's office was elective, not hereditary, as was that of the head of the rival state of Genoa.

Venice was a great power but its titular chief could hardly claim equality with the King of France or Spain. The title *Serenissimus* was taken for the far greater attribute (far greater, that is, than *Excellentissimus* or *Illustrissimus*), and one of the greatest that could be given to any prince who did not possess the supreme title of King. Thus at the treaty of Boulogne between the commissions of Queen Elizabeth I, the King of Spain, and the Archduke of Austria, one of several exceptions taken to the forms of the English commission was the use of *Illustrissimus*, as applied to the Archduke. The objectors pointed out that he was sprung from imperial ancestors, and had a brother who was King of Spain. In addition, he was married to the Infanta of Spain, Isabella, and these considerations entitled him to be called *Serenissimus*. After a good deal of argument, the title of Most Serene was accorded to the Archduke. The styles of Most Illustrious, Most Excellent, Most Powerful, Most Serene, and Most Exalted, have been variously given to subordinate dignitaries according to the fancies of the writers and the differences of ages and custom which govern most things in these matters. As Selden remarks, the Duke of Venice, who acknowledges no superior, does not use Majesty, but only Highness, or *Altezza* or *Celsitudo*.

The title of Duke, from its beginnings as the name of a Roman military commander, had spread widely. In the case of Venice and of Genoa, it was the title of the head of the state, like that of Stadtholder in republican Holland, but unlike the latter it did not become hereditary but remained elective. Most ducal titles in Europe developed into hereditary appendages, but their owners were generally subordinate in rank to the sovereigns of their respective countries. Thus the Great Dukes who for so long vexed the kingdom of France and prevented its cohesion were subject to the King of France. The Dukes of Britanny, Normandy, and Burgundy were technically vassals of the French monarch, who was their suzerain. In fact, his control over Britanny or Burgundy was very slight, at times almost non-existent. These exalted persons were the *pairs*, or peers, of the French Crown, whence comes our word, peer, though with a very different meaning in England. Most people will remember from their Shakespeare the trouble caused to France by the defection of the Duke of Burgundy to the English. Later in the fifteenth century, when the threat from England had died down and the English encroachment on French soil was limited to Calais, the Dukes of Burgundy pursued a course of action which appeared to aim at the elevation of their ducal coronet into a crown. They wished to become independent of their sovereigns.

One other case may be cited of a duke who was a supreme prince without an earthly superior. This was the Grand Duke of Muscovy, or Moscow. In Russian history we have the foundation of several principalities by the Swedish Vikings, foremost of whom was Rurik (*circa* 862), founder of the first Rus dynasty. In the course of some 500 years the Great Princes of Smolensk, Novgorod, Halicza and Kiev arose. Whoever among these was temporarily supreme thought himself overlord of the other Grand Princes. The Russians received their Christian culture from the Byzantines; by the thirteenth century they were in the same type of chivalric civilisation as their western compeers. All this way of life was overwhelmed by the invasions of the savage hordes of Mongols under their Khans. The latter title, yet another Turkish legacy, is derived from 'khaqan' or 'quhagan', meaning a ruler or sovereign, the form in Persian and Arabic being Khan. It was applied to the aptly named Hordes of Mongol horsemen, some of whom constituted the Golden Horde.* Anyone who has seen films of modern Mongolia, with its small population and backward condition, may well wonder at the effect which the ancestors of the modern Mongols had upon Europe and Asia. Temujin (born 1154), when he became the supreme ruler of the Mongols, assumed the title of Jenghiz Khan—the Very Mighty Lord. His successors, the Mongol Emperors of China, were known in Europe as the Great Khans, or Chams as it was corrupted. Coleridge and Marco Polo have made Kublai Khan a respected, almost kindly person. Very different, in fact, were Kublai's predecessors, whose favourite memorial was a huge pyramid of human skulls to show where their swords had been. They destroyed the brilliant Russian civilisation of Kiev, but spared some of the lesser princes; they entrusted the collection of tribute to the Grand Prince Vladi-

---

* The word 'Horde' (from Turkish) means 'camp', and the Golden Horde was supposed to derive its name from the golden tent of its chief, Batu, who became Great Khan in 1241. This body of Tartars was that of the West Kipchaks; the East Kipchaks were known as the White Horde.

71

mir. Eventually this right, which greatly strengthened the collector's position vis-a-vis the other princes, passed to the obscure Prince of Moscow. The title of Grand Prince (conferred by *yarlyk* or charter) was settled on the ruling house of Moscow from the early fourteenth century.

After the fall of Constantinople the Metropolitan of Moscow assumed the headship of the Orthodox church which had been previously subject to Byzantium. Under the Grand Prince Ivan III (1462-1505) not only was the area of the Muscovite state greatly enlarged but the Tartar yoke was thrown off. The Tartars' correct name was 'Tatar', a Turkish and Persian word, but the 'r' was inserted by Europeans who rightly regarded them as fiendlike and therefore come from Tartarus, or the classical hell. They remained a divided menace broken into three Hordes, of Kazan, Crimea and the Golden. The first of these was forced to pay tribute to the Duke, or Prince of Moscow. In 1472 Ivan married Sophia Paleologue, the niece of the last eastern emperor, Constantine XI. Thereafter Ivan made himself head of the church, assumed the double-headed eagle of Byzantium and the titles of Autocrat and Tzar (Czar). In his letters to foreign potentates (but not to the King of Poland) he used the style of Tzar. Apparently the Polish king refused to recognise any new title and would accept letters and embassies only from the Great Duke of Muscovy.

The nobles of old Russia were called 'boyars', being the holders of the chief offices of state. Their position was completely changed by Peter the Great, from whose time nobility was dated from the entries in the Red Book. The present whereabouts of this Muscovite *Burke's Peerage* is not known but doubtless it has been reverently preserved by the Soviet authorities along with other relics of Tzardom.

Another personage who haunted the minds of medieval thinkers, and still conjures up for us associations of distant romance, was the legendarily famous Prester John. He was located in various unknown Asiatic lands, possibly by confusion with some Nestorian (ie, heretical) Christian rulers. When the Nestorian Christians were driven from the Roman Empire they spread through Persia across central Asia as far as China. There may well have been small tribes or nations who were Nestorian Christians. The travels of Marco Polo dispelled the idea of a great Christian state in Asia, while the opening of the eastern ocean routes by the Portuguese brought to the knowledge of Europe the existence of Christian Ethiopia surrounded by a swarm of Islamic states. The Negus, or King of the Kings of Ethiopia, whom we call the Emperor, was identified with Prester John, that is Presbyter or Priest John, this ruler being reputed to be sacerdotal as well as regal. According to Selden, the term should really be 'Precious John', from an Ethiopian word meaning 'high' or 'lofty'.

In mentioning the style of Grand Duke for the potentate who became the Russian Caesar, we should observe the comparative title of Archduke found in Austria in the last few centuries, though examples of its use can be produced from earlier periods. It means literally 'chief duke', but in fact it has never been other than a title of eminent honour and did not imply superiority over other dukes. It is not clear when the title began to be used by the Austrian dukes and princes but it was established by the time of our Elizabeth I. It does not correspond to the usage of 'Arch' as in Archbishop, where the holder of that office has often an authority over other bishops. The first Duke of Austria was so created in 1156 by the Emperor Frederick I. In Italy, the Dukes of Florence were known as the Grand, or Great Dukes of that city. The first to be so created, by a Bull of Pope Pius V in 1569, was Cosmo di Medici, who was styled *Magnus Dux Etruriae*.

Proceeding to the grade below a duke, we should, in the modern order of rank, come next to a marquess but as this has already been described and actually developed from the office of a *comes*, or count, the latter ought to receive attention now. The title of *comes* evolved from an office which gradually developed into an hereditary position. For ages it was annexed to a function, that of ruling or administering an area, a county. In many old writings, eg, Shakespeare's *All's Well That Ends Well*, the Count is spoken of as 'County', a reminder of the fact that a count was not the bearer merely of a title of honour, but also had a task to perform. In England the Count was entitled to the third penny of the revenues in the form of fines and feudal dues in the county court. It was not until the close of the middle ages that the title of count was divorced from any feudal or territorial connection. Prominent among the title holders were the Counts of the Holy Roman Empire. In England, the old territorial connection is maintained still in the form of the title—as with Baron Smith of Reading in the county of Berkshire who does not possess even a flat in that area—and so it has been for a long time with the higher title of earl. On the Continent, the principle that all members of a noble family are noble has resulted in a deluge of *comtes, conti* and the like whose noblesse is almost impossible to check, owing to the disappearance of most European monarchies and the consequent dissolution of their chancellories and heraldic offices.

In medieval Europe, however, the privileges of the nobles were hardly earned. They were required to underprop the throne and feudal duties were rigorously exacted. Even a king had often to do homage to another king, not necessarily *qua* king but in virtue of a lesser dignity which one sovereign could hold of another. This is clear from the history of the Duke of Normandy who became King of England and yet had to render homage for his dukedom to his liege lord, the King of France. It is not always clearly realised that the original *casus belli* in the Hundred Years War between France and England consisted in the feudal necessity for the English king to render homage to his liege for his Aquitanian and Gascon lands. To be free of this obligation was Edward III's object and when, at the Treaty of Bretigny in 1360 he secured complete ownership of his French lands he agreed to drop the claim to the throne of France which he had made since 1340. Similarly, the relationship between the Scots king and his English counterpart is always complicated in the period before the Treaty of Northampton (1328) because the Scots king held lands in England not as a king but as a great noble, and for this property he had to do homage to the English monarch. The same was true of many of the great Scots lords, like the family of Bruce.

A medieval countship was, then, always attached to a territorial position. The same phenomenon is found in all the nations of Western Europe. In the Romance countries, *comes* is translated into the semi-Latin which proves the derivation of their tongues from the language of old Rome. In England, as usual, a compromise was made, with the (native) earl and his (continental) countess. In German we have *graf*, female *gräfin*. The German title of landgrave was applied to one of these great territorial *graves*, of whom in the medieval empire there were four : Thüringen, Hesse, Elsatz, and Luchtenburg.* The term implied the territory of the *graf* but as, under the empire, every *graf* was a territorial lord, the landgrave could only be a *graf* of outstanding power, cf. duke and archduke.

* Spellings are as given in Selden.

74

Burggrave was a title which applied to the *graf* of a castle or other fortified place.

In the modern peerage, the title and rank of viscount comes between count (earl) and baron. In origin, the viscount was the *vice comes*, ie, in place of the count. He was the count's deputy. As Selden observes: 'The beginning of this dignity (as it became feudal and hereditary) was in the like kind of divers counts. When the great dukes and counts in the ancient times gained to themselves large dominion . . . which was afterwards transmitted to their heirs, divers of them placed in certain towns and divisions of their counties, such governors and delegates under them' who likewise made their dignities descend to their heirs. In the time of Charlemagne and his immediate successors the *vice comites* held office by delegation from the counts. Very early in the tenth to the eleventh century the viscounts had become hereditary, always with the feudal connection of territory. The Normans used the title, especially, as the Norman dukes were at first counts (even William the Conqueror, before becoming King of England, was often termed Count of the Normans). After the Norman Conquest, the Normans gave the title of viscount to the English sheriff, but this usage did not last long. At first, then, like all the European titles, that of viscount denoted a real post and function; gradually it ceased to be such, and by 1440, in England, we have the creation of a viscount (John, Lord Beaumont), whose title is purely honorary. It need hardly be remarked that viscount has long ceased to be a title of office or position.

The office of the sheriff was at one time in England very important; probably it would not be untrue to say that it bore at least some resemblance to the mode of exercise with which most people are familiar from seeing western films. The sheriff of an English county under Alfred the Great would certainly have found a great deal of hard and dangerous work to do. In the event of an invasion by the Vikings, the sheriff's duty would be to lead the local soldiers to fight against the invaders. He had many administrative duties in addition. With the coming of the Normans, the importance of the sheriff declined, and although the title has continued to the present his functions are now much more honorary than important. Holding the office can be expensive, in view of social commitments, but the tenure is only for a year, and it is usually considered to be a great honour to have the position. In many cases the sheriff is referred to as High Sheriff. His name is taken from a panel of three which is submitted to the sovereign, who then pricks one of the names. A sheriff must have a banner of his arms, and a good deal of trouble can arise in this connection if the new sheriff has been using arms to which he is not entitled, as he will then have to take out a grant in a hurry. The sheriff, like the county, is one of Britain's legacies to the United States.

The title of constable is known to everyone from its huge extension in the British police force. Like many other titles of this kind it has a long and distinguished ancestry. It began at the Byzantine court, where the *comes stabuli* (in Greek Κόμης Τοῦ σταβλοῦ) was master of the horse. It was taken over in the Frankish kingdom, and there began to have a higher significance, meaning in later centuries that the holder was commander of the royal forces. The French kings did not allow the office to become hereditary, and abolished it in 1627. In England it was hereditary until the execution of the Duke of Buckingham, of the House of Stafford, who perished through the jealousy of Cardinal Wolsey. Thereafter the office of constable or high constable has been granted only for a short period, eg, at a coronation. In Scotland, the office still continues to be hereditary, being held in the family of Hay, headed by the Countess of Erroll, who is the High Constable for Scotland and as such has precedence in Scotland immediately after the blood royal.

The lowest order of the modern peerage is that of baron. It has fallen greatly from its ancient position, certainly in England where it was more or less a class term for the great nobles, as in the well-known title, *The Last of the Barons*, referring to the Earl of Warwick, Richard Neville. In olden days in feudal Europe, the barons were the great tenants of the crown. In the German empire, the barons were the *herren* or lords, and there were six classes of them, *freyen, liberi,* or freemen; *freyherren, liberi domini; semper freyen* or *semper liberi; herren, domini,* or lords; *edlen herren, nobiles domini; edlen aut nobiles.* Memories of the Herren Volk! Yet even among their ancestry there must have been glimpses of feudal, knightly chivalry.

What is the meaning of the word 'baron'? Simply from Old French and low Latin, *baro,* a man. This might seem a very commonplace meaning for a word once of such great importance, until we add to the *baro,* a man, the words, 'of the king'. Thus expressed,

76

we realise the significance of the title, the king's man, one of the great feudatories, or tenants of the crown. When William the Conqueror surveyed his new-won kingdom in Domesday Book (1086) he had let out the lands not immediately part of the royal demesne to about 180 tenants-in-chief. These were the great barons of the Crown, and their jealousies, struggles and treasons make up much of English history over the next 400 years. The process by which modern business men seek protection against the chill winds of competition was also employed among the medieval baronage. By careful marriage alliances, the barons had succeeded in reducing their numbers to some forty, most of whom were related to the royal house. Ultimately their rapacity and selfishness recoiled upon themselves and they lost their power in the Wars of the Roses. Some of their families were destroyed then; many more perished through the skilful arts of Henry VII and Henry VIII, whose upstart origins and real statecraft could brook no proud or over-mighty subjects. So it has happened that, in comparison with a king-making baron of old, the modern baron, holder probably of only a life peerage, is more like the harmless little iguana of our epoch than its relatives the gigantic reptiles of pre-human times. Power and potentiality for harm have gone, leaving the modern baron only the position of a prime minister's nominee.

From this outline it will be clear that all five titles of nobility represented in the British peerage are derived from actual offices or functions, but in process of time have become solely and simply titles of honour. The British titled system is the most interesting at present because it is the only one still in operation. It is always being threatened, laughed at or criticised, but many of its most strenuous ridiculers end by accepting its rewards. The more it changes, the more it remains in being. Very few other countries still possess a system of honours and titles. In Spain, the honours system is existent but dormant; in Sweden it is in perpetual suspension. In Britain, it operates to the extent of over 4-5,000 new awards each year.

NOTE : There was also reckoned among the imperial titles that of Wojewoda. The Vaivoda (as it was sometimes rendered by western writers) of Walachia, and the Vaivoda of Moldavia are mentioned as great dignitaries. In Poland the title was not at all feudal, nor to be reckoned among titles of honour but of offices. In the famous Polish poem, *Pan Tadeusz* by Adam Mickiewicz (Everyman Edition, p 77) there is the following passage: 'To be sure, Zosia will not be a wealthy match but yet she is not a common village girl, a simple gentleman's daughter; her ancestors were called "Your Grace"; her mother was a Horeszko; she will get a husband!' On this the poet has added a note: 'Joseph, Count Niesiolwski, the last Wojewoda of Nowogrodik, was president of the revolutionary government during Jasinki's insurrection.' On this the translator has added a further note. 'A wojewoda was the chief dignitary of a Polish province or wojewodeship. The office had very slight duties, and was rather a title of distinction than an administrative position. It was particularly valued because it conferred a seat in the senate.' This title is mentioned in passing as it had its origin under the Empire.

8. The Monarchies of Western Europe

From ancient times until the end of the French monarchy, the King of France was always styled the Most Christian King. The origin of this attribute is quite uncertain, but the old national legend was that it was bestowed on Clovis, the first Christian King of France and the first Catholic Christian monarch in Western Europe. The French king was also called, at least by his own people, the eldest son of the church. The exact differentiation between the French style and that of the Spanish sovereign is not clear. From early times the Kings of Spain (or rather the Kings of Castile and Aragon) used the attribute of Catholic, thus: The Catholic King, His Catholic Majesty. After the upheaval of the Reformation, the style of Catholic King was understandable enough for the King of united Spain, for while the Empire, France and other lands were in dispute between Protestants and Catholics, the Iberian peninsula was remarkably free from the taint of heresy. In addition to these titles sanctioned by the Popes through long usage, if not actually granted by the pontiffs, there were the titles of *Defensor Ecclesiae*, borne very often by the Emperor, and *Defensor Fidei* granted to the English King, Henry VIII, in 1521. Of the latter, more when dealing with English regal styles.

The eldest son of the King of France was called the Dauphin, a title derived from the province of Dauphiné. The term 'Dauphin' was a personal name to begin with, which became the title of the Counts of Vienne. In 1349 Humbert II, the last of the counts and dauphins of the area, sold his dominions to Charles of Valois, later Charles V, King of France, who in 1364 gave it to his eldest son, who henceforth bore the title of Dauphin. At first the actual territory (now the departments of Isere, Drome and Hautes-Alpes) was the land granted in each generation to the heir to the French Crown,

79

but after 1456, when Dauphiné was taken over by the Crown, the title of Dauphin described only the eldest son of the French king. The other sons were called simply Monsieur, followed by their Christian names; if they had an appanage, kingdom, dukedom, or the like, they put the style thus : King of Jerusalem, etc, son of the King of France, Count of Anjou etc.

After the King's sons, the immediate heirs to the Crown, came the other possible successors to the kingdom, being uncles, cousins of the sovereign. They were the Princes of the Blood and enjoyed many privileges in power, position and title, the nearest to the King being called, *Premier Prince du Sang*. The title of Princes of the Blood was peculiar to the French royal house, but as a general description of royal kinsmen it has passed into English usage and probably into other languages also. Henry III of France made an edict by which the precedence of the Princes of the Blood over other princes and *Seigneurs Pairs* of France was clearly established. Other princes were illegitimate issue of the royal family, who could not of course succeed to the throne, and therefore were not called Princes of the Blood, although manifestly they were of the blood royal.

Apart from the great dukes and counts who were found in France as in other European lands, there were some of supereminent position who were called *Pairs* or Peers, of France. These Peers of the Crown who proved themselves an almost unmitigated nuisance to the medieval French monarchy were twelve in number, six lay and six ecclesiastical. The lay peers were the Dukes of Guyenne, Burgundy and Normandy, and the Counts of Flanders, Toulouse, and Champagne. The dukedoms of Guyenne and Normandy were long in dispute with the English—Henry V's greatest achievement in France was the subjugation of Normandy. Burgundy was a menace to the stability of the French Crown, which it nearly overturned. The ecclesiastical peers were the Archbishop of Rheims, and the Bishops of Laon, Langres, Beauvois, Chalons, and Noyons. These Peers of France were associated with the monarchy in the government of the kingdom, and thus imposed a severe restraint upon the free action of the Crown. It should also be recalled that those great lords who were not formally Peers of the Crown, often possessed vast powers. Among these was the Duke of Brittany who exercised many royal powers, even to the extent of creating nobles. Thus in 1433, Jean V, Duke of Brittany, made Jean de Beaumanoir, Seigneur de Boys, de la Motts and de Tremeretto. The tenour of the letters under which these titles were granted is completely regal. The Duke refers to himself as being by the grace of God, Duke of Brittany, Count of Montfort and so on, and refers to his subjects and his princely rights.

As late as the reign of Louis XI, the Duke of Burgundy thought of raising his ducal coronet into a kingly crown, with a kingdom stretching from the Mediterranean to the North Sea. The death of this duke, the rash Charles the Bold, son of the famous Philip the Good, in battle at the hands of the Swiss brought all these schemes to an abrupt end.

At the French Revolution all French titles of honour and of nobility were abolished. As with so many other institutions destroyed by the *sans culottes*, nobility returned with Napoleon. Emperor of the French in 1804, he soon surrounded himself with a new nobility, much as Cromwell had created an Other House to replace the Lords whom the Puritans had abolished. Napoleon's nobility consisted of princes, dukes, counts, barons, and chevaliers, and these titles were recognised by the restored Bourbon king, Louis XVIII. The old nobility of the *ancien regime* and that of the First Empire were mingled in a new system in which all peerages were hereditary. Further changes took place in 1830, and a second abolition of peerages occurred in the 1848 revolution, to be followed by a revival under the Second Empire of Napoleon III. The frequent revolutions in France and the changing political conditions have made the titled system extremely complicated. To add to the difficulties, no book exists which gives anything but a partial view of the French (or for that matter any Continental nobility). This is no blame to the authors of such works, because they labour under two insurmountable obstacles. Very few countries in the world now maintain any record of their nobility; and because in the Continental systems every member of a noble family is noble, the multitude of titles is too great to be enumerated.

In Spain, the heir to the throne bore the title of Prince of the Asturias, or Prince of Spain. John I, King of Castile, had a son Henry, afterwards King Henry III, who in 1397 married Lady Katharine, the daughter of John of Gaunt. The prince was styled Prince of the Asturias. The eldest son of the King of Spain was also called Prince of Spain, and *Infante* (the last being used of the younger sons also, and *Infanta* for each daughter). *Alteza*, or Highness, was used only of the heir to the throne, otherwise the royal princes and princesses were styled *Senor el Infante Don X* or *Senora la Infanta Donna X*.

The roll of the titles of the Catholic king was necessarily very long owing to the fact that Spain was united only after many centuries of struggle between the various Spanish kingdoms, and with the Moors. It is what we could have expected in England if the Heptarchy had gradually come to unity by marriage and conquest. Here is an opening from an instruction on titles by Philip II in 1586.

'Don Philip by the Grace of God, King of Castile, of Leon, of Aragon, of the two Sicilies, of Jerusalem, of Portugal, of Navarre, of Granada, of Toledo, of Valentia, of Galicia, of Mallorcas, of Seville, of Cerdenna, of Cordova, of Corcega, of Murcia, of Jaen, of the Algarves, of Algecira, of Gibraltar, of the Isles of the Canaries, of the Indies, Eastern and Western, Isles and terra firma of the Ocean Sea, Archduke of Austria, Duke of Burgundy, of Brabant, and Milan, Count of Habsburg, of Flanders, of Tirol, and of Barcelona, Senor of Vizcaya, and of Molina etc.'

In this over-impressive list of kingly titles there is an enumeration of kingdoms which have formed the realm of Spain. With such an exordium to greatness it was only to be expected that the most exact attention should be given to the grades of nobility. *Duque* (duke) and *conde* (count) were used in Spain from the days when it was a Roman province, through the VisiGothic era until modern times. *Marques* (marquess) was used anciently, as Selden says, so nearly equivalent to *dux* and *comes* that it was distinguished from them by reason that the province over which the *marques* presided was that of a march or frontier. *Visconde* (viscount) had the same origin in Spain as elsewhere and all the above titles began as functional and continued as honorary hereditary distinctions. The title of baron is used in the Spanish nobility.

In olden days in Spain the title of the great feudal lords was *rico hombre*, a title of dignity. *Hombre rico* means a rich man, but *rico hombre* denotes one who had dependents and soldiers under him. Like the use of baron in medieval England, *rico hombre* could be used of a *conde*, as if it included the greater rank. There was a ceremony for the creation of a *rico hombre* in which the king granted him a banner and a cauldron. The former was a testimony of the power given to him to lead in war; the latter signified his ability to feed and support his vassals. The same ancient title was found among the Portuguese.

The *caballeros* or knights of Spain, like the rest of medieval chivalry, were the original stock of knighthood, from which evolved the military monastic orders of the country. There were three : St James of Compostella, of Alcantara, and of Calatrava. They still continue as orders in Spain. The untitled gentry of Spain are known as *hidalgos* and their class as *hidalguia,* meaning nobility, or gentry. It follows that all persons belonging to this class are armigerous. In modern Spain there is considerable research devoted to the subject and all orders and distinctions of honour are maintained with scrupulous care. Thus, to be recognised as belonging to the *hidalguia* it is necessary to prove this condition in a plea brought before the Royal Chancellery (Valladolid, Oviedo, Granada, and Pamplona) in the corresponding *Sala de los Hijosdalgo* (the sons of the nobles). All the lesser (ie, untitled) gentry of Spain base their genealogies on these pleas.

Finally Spain has bequeathed to the world, a word peculiarly expressive of the Hispanic attitude to nobility, grandee. What is the grandeeship *(grandeza)*? The titled nobility is of two classes, the grandees and those who do not possess *grandeza*. The grandees are those Spanish nobles of the highest rank, mainly of very great antiquity, whose positions were confirmed by Charles V in 1520. The titles of the nobility, *duque* etc, can be conferred without the *grandeza*. One of the privileges of the most eminent among the Spanish grandees was that of remaining covered in the presence of their sovereign. Only one British subject has ever claimed a similar privilege, the Lord de Courcy, head of an obscure noble house in Ireland, and for the foundations of this asserted privilege there is not even the doubtful support of legend.

There has not been among the Spaniards the modesty which has so far prevented a Briton from taking the title of Lord Atlantic or Earl of the Grampians. When a Spanish novelist satirised his country, making a noble *duque* of the Atlantic, this was not a very great departure from many of the titles current among Hispanic nobility. Even an upstart like the famous Christopher Columbus put in a claim to the title of Grand Admiral of the Ocean Sea (ie, the Atlantic Ocean), with a vice-royalty of all lands discovered by him, plus ten per cent of the value of the commerce of these lands. Count of the Andes is a style not unknown in Spain. On the other hand, the riches and greatness in a material sense of the Spanish grandees have to be seen to be understood.

The nobility of Germany is varied to a degree which can be confusing, because of the country's division into separate principalities and kingdoms, each of which had its own orders of nobility. *Graf*, as we have seen, corresponds to the *comes* as the latter term was carried over into the languages derived from Latin. Baron was much used in Germany, but duke was rendered *herzog*. More difficult to the English reader is the use of the title Prince. In England it has the meaning of a royal highness, a member of the royal family. A duke in England can be referred to as 'high and mighty prince', but this is only an historical accident derived from the fact that, long ago, dukes were once related to the royal house. In Germany, the great feudatories of the Crown (the tenant-in-chief as would be said in England) were termed Princes (Fürst). As might be expected in the course of centuries, the number of princes was restricted, until only those who were entitled to sit in the Diet of the Empire were called by this title. At length, in the thirteenth century, the college of princely electors set itself up as the body which chose the emperor. During the seventeenth and eighteenth centuries the number of German principalities increased with a corresponding enlargement in the number of princes. However, as so often happens, increase in one era spells reduction in the next. With the abolition of the empire, there were many princes whose position had been sovereign because they held immediately of the emperor. On the removal of their suzerain, they lost their sovereignty and were placed under other rulers, from whom they were said to hold their fiefs mediately. This is the process known as mediatisation and the sovereigns thus reduced are known as the mediatised princes. Sir Bernard Burke in one of his now out of print works, *Reminiscences Ancestral and Anecdotal*, p 241, gave a list of German mediatised families under two heads: (i), Princes of the Holy Roman Empire (the junior members bearing the title of count), and (ii), Counts of the Holy Roman Empire who formerly possessed sovereign rights. He adds that all the houses which held directly and immediately of the empire are all considered upon an equality as to blood, 'and an Emperor of Austria may, if he please, choose an Empress from the Bentincks, Fuggers, Platens-Walmodens, Wurmbrands etc.'

Perhaps it may not be amiss in this connection to explain the meaning of a morganatic marriage, which is a perfectly legal union

84

between a member of a reigning or mediatised family and someone of lesser rank. The wife does not bear the family name, arms or title of her husband; the children, though legitimate, cannot inherit their father's titles or entailed property. The word 'morganatic' is from the German, *morgen* or morning, since the bride receives only a gift on the morning after the wedding. At one stage in the abdication controversy of Edward VIII, the suggestion was put forward that he should marry Mrs Simpson morganatically, ie, she would be his wife but not his Queen. At once the old familiar cry was raised that such a marriage was unknown to the British constitution, the implication being that it was therefore out of the question. Strangely, though, after the King's abdication and subsequent marriage, his wife was deprived of the usual style of Her Royal Highness, an arrangement quite unknown to British procedure whereby a wife always shares in her husband's title, but which savours strongly of morganatic practice.

There were also in Germany and Austria princes of lesser rank than the Princes of the Empire, who were called 'Serene Highness', in this way conforming to the proposition advanced by Selden to account for cases like that of Monaco, where a prince of lower rank than the greater royalties yet had his susceptibilities assuaged by the designation of Serene. *Prinz* (ie, Fürst) was reserved for the non-reigning members of a sovereign house. *Kronprinz* was the heir to the throne, *Erbgrossherzog*=hereditary grand duke, and *Erbprinz* =hereditary prince. When the heir to Prussia was not the son of the reigning monarch, he was called *Prinz von Preussen* (Prince of Prussia), a style which will recall to many the name by which Kaiser Wilhelm II's grandson, the late Mr Mansfield, was known in England. Even before the process of mediatisation, some of the sovereign princes ranked, as in monarchical France, below a duke.

In Italy, a very large number of noble titles existed, again for the same reason as in Germany, that the country had been divided into so many separate states. The range of titles was the usual to be found in European lands—*principe, duca, marchese, conte, visconte, barone, signore, nobile, patrizio* and *cavaliere*. These were all hereditary and the nobility and patricianate formerly existed in every self-governing city. In the papal states, where the Popes ruled for over 1,000 years as temporal sovereigns until 1870, the titles were as mentioned for other Italian states but with the addition of *coscritto* as the lowest. Papal titles still continue to be created, and every Pope

85

has a coat of arms, at least after his elevation. In the instance of Pope John XXIII, the escutcheon dated back some three or four centuries (see his book, *The Journal of a Soul*, 1965, p 476). Papal titles are not recognised in England (see second note below).

The word 'prince' was formerly used on a very wide scale to describe anyone who was a sovereign ruler. An outstanding example is *Il Principe* by Niccolo Machiavelli (1513), in which he refers to any and every sovereign ruler by this title. The work is dedicated : *Al Magnifico Lorenzo di Piero de Medicii*, the dukedom of Florence not beginning in this family until later.

NOTE 1. Russian nobility. To the details already given concerning the boyars the following can be added. Russian thought on the subject of nobility and heraldry has been modelled on that of the west. The princes of Russia came from three sources. They were descended from the original Viking rulers, scions of the House of Rurik; from the Jagellon dynasty of Poland and Lithuania; or from formerly ruling states whose domains had been annexed by the Russian Tzars. Later there were persons who were made princes, but who were not of the royal blood. Under the Tzar Theodore III (1676-82), the former rules regarding nobility were rescinded and all Russian noblemen were, by decree, given the same rights irrespective of their origin. Previously the princes of Russia had been brought to the level of the boyars and had all been inscribed in a register. Two families—of Adasheff and Guedemine—were added to the register under Ivan IV (1533-84). It was then also decided that the rank of nobility should be regulated by the position held, in either civil or military employment, by the father or other ancestors of each nobleman. This decree was known as *Mestnichestro*.

After 1682, the register was copied for the last time, and from its red velvet binding it came to be known as the Velvet Book. New names were not added to the record. Peter the Great (1689-1725), introduced the titles of princes, counts (1706) and barons (1710). In 1722 he ruled that all officers of the armed forces and civilian officials who had attained a certain rank should acquire hereditary nobility. He also began the use of armorial bearings in Russia. The five classes of Russian nobility were (1) princes, (2) counts, (3) barons, (4) gentlemen ennobled before the reign of Peter I, and (5) gentlemen ennobled after the reign of Peter I. The title of duke came in in 1890, when it was used for some legitimated members of the royal family.

NOTE 2. Foreign titles borne by British subjects. It has long been the rule that no British subject may accept a title from a foreign sovereign or use an hereditary title of foreign origin without the permission of the British sovereign. The sovereign is the sole Fountain of Honour within his or her dominions. In the reign of Elizabeth I there were several instances in which that Queen imprisoned those of her subjects who, without her consent, had accepted foreign titles. The outstanding case was that of Thomas, 1st Lord Arundell of Wardour, who had been allowed by Elizabeth to take part in the wars of the Emperor against the Turks. He showed such conspicuous bravery that the Emperor made him a Count of the Holy Roman Empire. On his return home he found not only the Queen furiously at odds with him, but public opinion also. The House of Lords made a formal representation against recognition of the title, and Lord Arundell was banished from court and committed to the Fleet prison. Elizabeth set out her objections in her own inimitable style: 'As chaste women ought not to cast their eyes upon any other than their own husbands, so neither ought subjects to cast their eyes up on any other prince than him whom God hath set over them. I would not have my sheep branded with another man's mark: I would not have them follow the whistle of a strange shepherd.' In after times some licences to use foreign titles were granted, but in the latter part of Queen Victoria's reign the rule was made that all such applications were to be refused, unless exceptional circumstances existed in which the Queen could be advised to accept them. This reflected the changed position of the sovereign, who no longer ruled directly but acted on the advice of her ministers.

In 1932 King George V issued a warrant which he directed to be enrolled in the College of Arms—it is of course addressed to 'Our Right Trusty and Right Entirely Beloved Cousin Bernard Marmaduke, Duke of Norfolk, Earl Marshal and Our Hereditary Marshal of England.' The warrant sets out that, in the royal opinion, it is expedient for the use in this country of foreign titles of nobility to cease, but that there are exceptions to the principle, so that some licences can be continued for two or three generations. There were thirty-one names in the schedule attached to the warrant, and the titles were mostly those of the Holy Roman Empire, being in the families of the Duke of Portland (Bentinck) and De Salis. Omissions from the schedule were sometimes as surprising as the contents. However, the position is perfectly clear: apart from the titles set out in this schedule, no British subject can bear a foreign title without the permission of the Crown and such permission will not be given, unless circumstances at the time of the application were greatly changed. The name of Arundell of Wardour is not in the schedule!

There has been about this warrant a delightful air of mystery of the kind which some people love to encounter, but which is rather boring for those who are concerned with facts. After the second world war, when my task was to clear up *Burke's Peerage*, I found a large Foreign Titles section. In order to deal adequately with this, I sought advice. I heard of the warrant of 1932, but was advised that it ought not to be published. Why not? Some years later I was even asked to visit the Home Office where I received a briefing on the matter and much useful advice, but still no publicity was desired. It is a strange position. Nothing has occurred since 1932 to alter the terms of the warrant, but apparently out of consideration for some who hold foreign honours, the matter must be kept *sub rosa*.

Perhaps it need not be added that titles emanating from the Pope have never been accepted by British sovereigns, at least not since the reign of James II. This is a little unfortunate for those whose names we read from time to time as having received a distinguished order of knighthood from the Pope. They cannot use the title of 'Sir' nor can their wives be 'Lady'; they must wait upon the receipt of a plain knight bachelorship from Elizabeth II.

9. The English Royal Styles

In writing of the monarchies of Europe the past tense has very often to be used. Although ten monarchies survive in Europe—beside the British, there are those of Sweden, Norway, Denmark, Greece, Holland, Belgium, Liechtenstein, Luxembourg and Monaco—only in Britain does a monarch preside even nominally over a great power. A writer may therefore treat separately of the British monarchy without being accused of chauvinism. Indeed, to the present writer, there is something most melancholy in recounting the story of the English sovereign's ascent in greatness. For do we not now witness the reverse of this progress, a veritable descent into the heptarchical depths of pettiness from which arose the once greatest empire in history? Perhaps it is the suddenness of the change which makes the the story all the more gloomy. In 1939 the British Empire was still intact, save for the defection of the twenty-six counties of southern Ireland.

Out of the Roman province of Britain there came, after the darkness of two unrecorded centuries, a welter of small kingdoms, the Heptarchy, each with its royalty descended from Woden or Odin, the supreme god of our pagan ancestors. One dynasty of Saxon kinglets, that of Essex, took its origin from Saxnot, possibly an older god, or divinized hero, than Woden. These kingdoms warred with each other and the one which held supremacy secured to its monarch the title of Bretwalda, or ruler of the Britons, a curious title for a Saxon chief. Probably, even at this early date, he whose overlordship was acknowledged by other Saxons assumed that the British or Welsh kinglets would subscribe likewise.

In the second half of the eighth century the king of one of the larger states, Mercia, roughly the equivalent of the present English midlands, rose to pre-eminence. King Offa reigned from 757 to 796 and held the position of Bretwalda, however, shadowy it might have been in actual power. His control over England did extend in a very real way to the Channel, for we find grants made by him and other indications of his direct influence in places on the Sussex coast. He corresponded on equal terms with Charlemagne. In one of Offa's official documents occurred the famous phrase, *Rex totius Anglorum patriae*, King of all England. Some thirty years after Offa's death, the supremacy had passed to Egbert of Wessex, an ancestor of Elizabeth II, who is his sixty-second successor. It was Egbert's grandson, Alfred, who alone of England's kings has deserved the title of 'The Great'. He saved England from being overrun by the Danes, and he fought them to a standstill, thus preserving the independence of England and providing his successors with a secure base from which to begin the recovery and unification of the whole country. Alfred's son, Edward I, the Elder,* reigned as overlord of most of Britain. His son, Athelstan, was styled in his charters *Rex totius Britanniae*, and used the Greek title of Basileus, a development highly significant of the power and position of the Old English kings. Edgar, who reigned 959-75, was recognized as King of all England, and styled himself Emperor of Britain. The ceremony in which he was rowed on the Dee at Chester by seven tributary kings was indicative of his status. His coronation took place at Bath in 973 and the *ordo* used in this religious consecration of his kingship is the foundation of that used to the present time.

With the intrusion of the Danish line of kings, England was linked with Norway and Denmark, Canute being ruler of all three countries. One of the two sons who succeeded him, Hardicanute, was King of England and of Denmark. The English line was restored with Edward III—the Confessor—but terminated when his successor, Harold II, was defeated and killed at Hastings in 1066.

William the Conqueror began a new succession of kings, but was determined to appear as the legal successor to Edward the Confessor. He was therefore styled *Willelmus Rex Anglorum*, besides being, of course, *Dux Normaniae*. He enforced upon the Welsh princes and the King of Scots the same rights of suzerainty as had been claimed and exercised by the Old English kings and accepted by the Scots kings. Andrew Lang, in his *History of Scotland* (1907, vol i, pp 168-9) argues ingeniously that the overlordship of England was not received by the Scots. A case is always bad when instance

---

* The numbering of the Old English kings (three Edwards before the Conquest) was not continued after 1066.

after instance in a long succession has to be explained away. The Scots gained recognition of their independence at the Treaty of Northampton 1328, only to have it compromised time and again by Scottish monarchs and Scottish nobles eager for the feel of 'the bonny English siller'. Before the time of Edward I (1272-1307), the English sovereigns were the feudal superiors of the Scots. William the Conqueror was far too legally minded to have trumped up a claim unknown to his English predecessors.

William II—Rufus—was styled *Dei Gratia Rex Anglorum*, as was his brother and successor, Henry I. In the titles of the three Norman sovereigns we have the use of the phrase, King of the English, not of England, in line with the usage in France and elsewhere.

After the death of Henry I in 1135 comes the period known as the Anarchy, when Henry's daughter, Matilda, and his nephew, Stephen, contended for power. Matilda's style is of particular importance as she is the first woman sovereign of England. She was called : *Matildis Imperatrix Henrici Regis filia et Anglorum Domina* —Maltilda, Empress, daughter of King Henry, and Lady of the English. The title of Empress was from her first marriage to the Emperor, Henry V, and she was known as the Empress even after her second marriage, to the Count of Anjou. Her other title of Lady of the English may have been a reminiscence of the title of Alfred the Great's daughter, Ethelfleda, the Lady of the Mercians, who was married to the sub-king of Mercia.

Stephen's style was the same as that of Henry I, and in addition he was *jure uxoris* Count of Mortain and Boulogne. Matilda secured the succession to the throne for her son, Henry II, whose title was *Rex Angliae* (of England, for the first time), *Dux Normaniae, et Aquitainiae, et Comes Andigaviae*, the last being Anjou. The dukedome of Aquitaine and the English possessions in the west of France came through the marriage of Henry II with Eleanor of Aquitaine, the divorced wife of the King of France. For the next 300 years the possession of these French lands was to be a source of constant trouble to both England and France. Under Richard I, whose formal style was the same as Henry II's, we encounter the first of those foreign possessions outside continental Europe with which the English Crown has been so liberally endowed. Richard conquered Cyprus, and was called king of that country and of Jerusalem, though the latter could not have been more than a complimentary usage. In passing, it can be recalled that in the later part of his reign, Henry II had been able to invade Ireland, through permission of Pope Adrian IV—the only Englishman ever to sit in St Peter's chair—and in virtue of the submission of the Irish kings he became *Dominus Hiberniae*. It was probably because the new territory was looked upon as held of the Papacy that the title of *Dominus* was taken instead of the more normal *Rex*.

King John lost Normandy in 1204. The title of *Dux Normaniae* therefore dropped out of the royal style. From his time until that of Edward III, the English kings were styled *Rex Angliae, Dominus Hiberniae, et Dux Aquitainiae*. In 1340, in the thirteenth year of his reign, Edward III assumed the title of King of France, thus : *Dei Gratia, Rex Angliae et Franciae, et Dominus Hiberniae*. This was in pursuance of his claim in right of his mother to be King of France. The next two monarchs—Richard II and Henry IV—bore the same title. So did Henry V until 1421 when, following the Treaty of Troyes in 1420, he had been recognised by the French king as heir of France, and had married the King's daughter, Katharine. Henry V then no doubt felt that his aims had been achieved and adapted his regal title to suit the new situation. He was *Rex Angliae, Haeres et Regens Franciae et Dominus Hiberniae*. His only son, Henry VI, was styled *Dei Gratia Rex Angliae, et Franciae et Dominus Hiberniae*. He was the only English king ever to be crowned as King of France, an event which took place in Notre Dame on 17 December 1431. The title, King of France, remained as the official style of the English kings from 1340 to 1800, except for this short break when Henry V was Heir and Regent of France.

There was no change in the titles of our kings until the time of Henry VIII. Under this sovereign there occurred the vast upheaval of the English Reformation and the breach with the Papacy which, with the brief exception of the short reign of Queen Mary I (1553-58), has continued ever since. The national life was affected in every respect and not least in the sphere of the royal titles.

To begin with, Henry was a zealous Catholic who abhorred Martin Luther and all his reforms. Before the rise of Lutheranism, the King was addressed by Pope Julius II in 1513 by the express title of 'His Most Christian Majesty', but although often styled in this manner by foreign rulers and others, he did not employ the title in his own declarations. In 1521, after he had written a book against Luther and in defence of the Catholic faith, Pope Leo X gave him the title of *Fidei Defensor* : Defender of the Faith, which still appears on our coins and in the official style of our Queen. Less than twenty years later the English king had made allegiance to the Pope an offence, substituted himself as head of the Church of England and opened the doors for the entry of a new faith for his successors to defend. 'From about 1526 he added the word *Octavus* after his name. By Statute 26 Henry VIII, c.i, the king was declared "Supreme Head of the Church of England" and that addition was made to his style at a Council, 15 January, 26 Henry VIII. In 1542 a statute was passed in the Irish Parliament declaring that the King of England, his heirs and successors, should for the future be Kings of Ireland (Irish Stats. 33 Henry VIII, c.i.). This was confirmed by an English Act of 1543-44' (*English Historical Documents*, vol v, p 474.) Thus the title of Henry's predecessors for 400 years, Lord of Ireland, was changed without any fuss into that of King. So it remained until the Anglo-Irish Treaty of 1921.

In the English statute of 1543 referred to above, the King's titles are set forth in full detail. In Latin : *Henricus Octavus Dei Gratia, Angliae, Franciae, et Hiberniae, Rex, fidei Defensor, et in terra Ecclesie Anglicane et Hibernie supremum caput*, or in English : Henry the Eighth by the Grace of God, King of England, France and Ireland, Defender of the Faith, and of the Church of England and also of Ireland in earth the Supreme Head.

Anyone who in any way presumed to impugn this title was to be deemed guilty of high treason. Reference is also made in this Act to the Imperial Crown of this His Highness's realm of England. Taken in conjunction with a reference in another statute to the effect that the realm of England has always been an empire, subject to no earthly power, it emphasises the fact that this country had never been anything but an independent realm; never a part of the Holy Roman Empire.

In view of the vast changes indicated by the King's new titles, it was only natural for him to be addressed as His, or Your, Majesty, whereas his predecessors had been content with Highness or Sovereign Lord Highness. Indeed Henry VIII *was* Majesty, and ruled his country as no other sovereign before or after him. His will prevailed throughout the national life. The greatest innovation in his style was the claim to be Head on earth of the Church. In this he deliberately put himself in the place of the Vicar of Christ, the Pope.

When Henry died, he had the comforting knowledge that his matrimonial tangles had been worthwhile. He had achieved his object, to leave England with an heir, his son Edward VI. Henry's will allowed for the succession in turn of Edward, Mary and Elizabeth, should the earlier sovereigns prove issueless. Edward VI was styled the same as his father, so, too, was Mary I—Bloody Mary—until her marriage, by proxy, on 25 July 1554 to Philip, the Prince of Spain, the son of the Emperor Charles V, then contemplating the monastic calm to which he would retire after abdicating the following year. On the morning of the wedding Philip was given by his father the style of King of Naples and of Jerusalem, so that he should not be unequal with his bride. The royal couple were on a par, Philip was not a prince consort married to a queen regnant, but they were two sovereigns, and the acts of Mary's reign bear the name of King Philip as well as her own. 'Philip and Mary, by the Grace of God, King and Queen of England, and France, Naples, Jerusalem and Ireland, Defenders of the Faith, Princes of Spain and Sicily, Archdukes of Austria, Dukes of Milan, Burgundy and Brabant'. By the adoption of this duality, Mary, the devout and zealous Catholic, escaped the odium she would have incurred in describing herself as Supreme Head of the Church.

With Mary's death after a short, sad and disastrous reign, the whole of her counter-Reformation measures collapsed. Protestantism triumphed in the person of Elizabeth I, and as she resisted all attempts at marriage there was no marital change in her titles. With regard to the use by her father and brother of the claim to headship over the Church, Elizabeth showed from the start the consummate statecraft which was to guide all her actions. 'In the first public document of her reign an etc. was put at the end of the Queen's titles, where in her father's and brother's reigns the title of Supreme Head of the Church had been.' (*Queen Elizabeth*, by J. E. Neale, 1952, p 63.) By this means Catholics were left guessing, and yet Protestants and Erastians were given no direct denial of the headship. So for her own time and succeeding ages, Elizabeth I has been, 'Queen of England, France and Ireland, Defender of the Faith, etc.' She refused the title of Supreme Head of the Church and took that of 'governor' which does not imply an overriding power, but rather an administrative authority in accordance with established laws. She further explained that the supremacy of the Crown consisted in having the rule over all persons born within the Queen's realm, whether they were lay or ecclesiastical. 'Thus the constitutional character of the supremacy of the Crown was expressly vindicated by Elizabeth, very much in the same terms as it was explained by Henry VIII to the northern Convocation in 1531 and does not differ in principle from that exercised by William I or Edward I, being in its essence the right supervision over the administration of the church vested in the Crown as the champion of the church, in order that the religious welfare of its subjects may be duly provided for.' (*History of the Church of England*, by H. O. Wakeman, 1943, p 313.)

On the accession to the English throne of James VI of Scotland in 1603, the two crowns were united, but the two countries did not have a legislative union for another century. James was, therefore, styled King of England, Scotland, France and Ireland, Defender of the Faith, etc. This is familiar to many people from the dedication of the Authorized (1611) Version of the Bible, in which James is addressed as 'The Most High and Mighty Prince'. In the dedication he is referred to as 'Your Majesty and Your Highness.' James VI of Scotland was manifestly James I of England. The troubles over the use of the correct numeral lay some distance away.

No alteration occurred in the style of English sovereigns until the reign of William III and Mary II, which began in 1689. Here again, as with Philip and Mary I more than a century earlier, there are two consorts having equal sovereignty. William was by birth and inheritance Prince of Orange Nassau as well as Stadtholder of Holland, under the title of William III. The connection between Holland and Orange in Provence came about through the usual curious interweaving of European rulerships. Philibert of Orange-Chalon commanded with the Constable of Bourbon in 1527, when the troops of Charles V stormed and sacked Rome. On Philibert's subsequent death, his title and principality went to the son of his sister, Claude, who had married William of Nassau. The principality of Orange-Nassau then passed to René de Nassau. (*The House of Orange*, Marion E. Crew, 1947.) The fate of Orange was to be absorbed into France, but its name has lived on because of the greatness of at least two of its princes, William the Silent, and William III of England, last Prince of Orange. William and Mary bore the titles of King and Queen of England, Scotland, France and Ireland, Defenders of the Faith etc.

Meanwhile, the dethroned James II had gone to live in exile in

94

France under the protection of Louis XIV. Since James still claimed to be lawful king, there were in France after his arrival two persons bearing the title of King of France, but, as Macaulay remarks, the generosity of Louis was prepared to overlook the flouting of his royal arms on the shield of his pensionary.

Anne, who succeeded William and Mary, bore at first the same style, but after the Treaty of Union with Scotland in 1707 she was entitled Queen of Great Britain, France and Ireland, Defender of the Faith. On her death in 1714, her cousin, the great grandson of James I, George Louis, the Elector of Hanover, succeeded to the British throne. His title was King of Great Britain, France, and Ireland, Duke of Brunswick-Luneburg, etc, Defender of the Faith. This style lasted throughout the reign of his son, George II, and that of his great grandson, George III until 1801, when the titles of the last named were altered to allow for greatly changed circumstances. The Union of Great Britain and Ireland took place on 1 January 1801. The title of the King then became, 'By the Grace of God, of the United Kingdom of Great Britain and Ireland King, Defender of the Faith.' At last the 460-year old pretence of kingship over France was dropped.

The succeeding kings, George IV and William IV, bore the same titles as their father. With the succession of Queen Victoria, the possession of Hanover (by then a kingdom) passed to her uncle, Ernest, Duke of Cumberland, owing to the operation of the Salic Law, which in Hanover, as with other Continental countries, barred women from the throne. Victoria was styled the same as William IV until 1 January 1877 when the proud title of Empress of India was assumed. 'By the Grace of God, of the United Kingdom of Great Britain and Ireland, Queen, Defender of the Faith, Empress of India.'

The style of the British sovereign has altered in four out of the five reigns from Victoria to her great-great-granddaughter, Elizabeth II. The machinery for effecting these changes is by Act of Parliament, or by royal proclamation or Order in Council issued thereunder. The Royal Titles Act 1876 is described in its preamble as 'An act to enable Her most gracious Majesty to make an addition to the Royal Style and Titles appertaining to the Imperial Crown of the United Kingdom and its Dependencies.' It is mentioned that the Union with Ireland Act, 1800, had provided for an alteration to the royal style and titles by a royal proclamation under the

Great Seal of the United Kingdom. Under the Government of India Act, 1858, the Government of India previously vested in the East India Company had been vested in Her Majesty to be governed in her name. The transfer of the government should therefore be recognised by an addition to the style and titles of Her Majesty.

Short lived glory; little more than seventy years later another Act gave Parliament's assent to the omission of the words 'Emperor of India' from the sovereign's style. The dying remark of James V of Scotland after the birth of his daughter is even more appropriate to this case than to Scotland's. 'It came with a lass, it will go with a lass.'

On the accession of a new sovereign, Edward VII, there was again a new style, designed to recognise the enormous extension of the British Empire under the rule of his mother, the Great White Queen, whose name the most remote potentates of the earth had learned to revere. The Royal Titles Act, 1901, provided for the resounding style of Edward VII : By the Grace of God, of the United Kingdom of Great Britain and Ireland, and of the British Dominions beyond the Seas, King, Defender of the Faith, Emperor of India. In Latin it read thus—and what Roman Imperator could have boasted such a title roll— : *Edwardus Septimus, Dei Gratia Britanniarum et terrarum transmarinarum quae in ditione sunt Britannica Rex, Fidei Defensor, Indiae Imperator.* The title list represents the zenith of England's greatness; thereafter the decline was swift and irretrievable. No historian will be able to emulate for the fall of the British Empire the sonorous stately diction of Gibbon. Whereas Rome fell slowly and against the will of her citizens, Britain's fall from imperial status was accomplished in half a generation with the earnest goodwill of her nationals.

George V bore until 1927 the same style as Edward VII. In 1921 the Irish Free State had come into being, and, though classed as a dominion, was in reality an independent country. The words 'of Great Britain, Ireland and the British Dominions beyond the Seas', were substituted for 'the United Kingdom of Great Britain and Ireland etc.' This was the arrangement following the Imperial Conference of 1926 and the Royal and Parliamentary Titles Act, 1927.

Edward VIII inherited his father's style along with his throne for less than a year. He abdicated on 11 December 1936. His Majesty's Declaration of Abdication Act, 1936, stated that in pursuance of the King's Instrument of Abdication on 10 December, 'thereupon His Majesty shall cease to be King, and there shall be a demise of the Crown.' Accordingly, an event without precedent in British history then took place. The King Emperor lost at one stroke all his titles. What was he to be called? His brother and sovereign, the new king, George VI, solved Mr Edward Windsor's problem by creating him Duke of Windsor on 8 March 1937. His precedence came between his brothers, the Dukes of Gloucester and Kent; to his wife the style of H.R.H., accorded to himself, was denied.

George VI was called the same as his brother and father until 1947 when, by the Indian Independence Act of that date, the title of Emperor of India became redundant and was dropped from the royal style.

Under the Statute of Westminster, 1931, it is stated that 'it would be in accord with the established constitutional position of all the members of the Commonwealth in relation to one another that any alteration in the law touching the Succession to the Throne or the Royal Style and Titles shall hereafter require the assent as well of the Parliaments of all the Dominions as of the Parliament of the United Kingdom.'

With the accession of the present Queen, it was clearly essential that recognition should be given to the new entity, the Commonwealth, which had replaced the British Empire without even stopping to couple the qualification of British to its name. Her Majesty succeeded to the throne on 6 February 1952, when her father died suddenly. The Royal Titles Act, 1953, 'is the outcome of agreement reached at the Commonwealth Economic Conference held in London in December 1952 on the form of the Royal Style and Titles. Each country mentioned in the preamble to the Act is to adopt the style which best suits its own circumstances, but a substantial element is common to all, ie, the description of the Sovereign as Queen of Her other Realms and Territories and Head of the Commonwealth.' (*Halsbury's Statutes*, vol 33 p 28.) The countries mentioned are the United Kingdom, Canada, Australia, New Zealand, the Union of South Africa, Pakistan, and Ceylon. Of these seven, the last three have subsequently become republics. Her Majesty's title is then: Elizabeth II by the Grace of God, of the United Kingdom of Great Britain and Northern Ireland and of Her other Realms and Territories, Queen, Head of the Commonwealth, Defender of the Faith. The 'Head of the Comonwealth' is a vague term which implies no power of any kind. It is really a courtesy title, as inexplicable as the nature of the Commonwealth is indefinable.

What of the numeral II? Exception to this has been taken by Scots, because, they argue, no other Elizabeth has ever been Queen of Scotland. Similar objections were taken to the title of Edward VII. We can have some sympathy with Scots feeling for, after all, the names of Elizabeth and Edward are not the most pleasing to a patriotic northern ear.

In the first place, it is only after the Union of England and Scotland that the difficulty (from the Scots' viewpoint) arises. The Union of the Crowns in 1603 still did not do away with the separate identity of the countries and thus James VI of Scotland was James I of England, and his grandson James II of England was James VII of Scotland. After 1707, the succession of four Georges to the throne of Great Britain could raise no problem, since neither country had previously had kings of this name. The same applied to Queen Anne in the rest of her reign after the Union. On the advent of William IV to the throne, Scottish opposition might have been expected, but another century was to pass before Scots nationalism was sufficiently pronounced to become irritated by the numeral after the sovereign's name. Nothing came of the objection from some Scots to the numbering of Edward VII and so far as is known, no objection was ever raised to Edward VIII's numeral.

The position as regards Elizabeth II is that the sovereigns of the greater entity—the United Kingdom, the British Empire, call it what we will—have always taken their regal numeral from the race of sovereigns established at the Norman Conquest. The English are not as a race possessed of much historical imagination. If they were, they would long since have insisted that those of their sovereigns who bore the name of Edward should be correctly numbered. Three Edwards reigned before the Conquest, Edward the Elder (1), St Edward the Martyr (II), and St Edward the Confessor (III). According to some references given by Edward Freeman, the first Edward after the Conquest was styled *Edwardus Quartus*, but owing to the insipidities of courtiers and officials the correct numbering was displaced in favour of *Primus*. Thus the numeral succession of English sovereigns begins from William the First, the Conqueror. Accordingly, the ignorance of the English as regards dates in their history, hazy after 1066, becomes a positive darkness so far as all time before the Norman invasion is concerned. So the rich heritage of our history is overlooked and we forget that we are English folk, as so termed in the *Anglo-Saxon Chronicle*, not Danes or Normans. Even in a learned work (*The Principles of English Law and the Constitution*, O. Hood Phillips, 1939, p 229-30), we are misinformed. 'The number attached to the name of a King refers to the Kings of England since the Norman Conquest. Edward VIII would have been the ninth Edward if Edward the Confessor were included, but the second Edward if the numbers dated only from the Union with Scotland.'

The use, then, of the Second as numbering for our present Queen is an expression of nationalism, the more astounding as having come from the representatives of a downtrodden people.

In the Continental monarchies the practice has sometimes been similar to that in England. The Kings of Prussia, on becoming Emperors of Germany in 1871, ceased to use the numeral succession of their kingdom, William III of Prussia becoming William I of Germany. His son, William, was universally referred to as William II. In the case of the Tzars of Russia, after the time of Peter the Great, the enumeration sometimes followed on that of the Grand Dukes or Tzars of Moscow, sometimes not. When the kingdoms of Navarre and of France were united in 1607, Henry IV of France had been Henry III of Navarre, and his successors followed the numbering of the Kings of France, though only one Louis had reigned in Navarre. In Spain, where some half-dozen kingdoms were merged into one realm, the numbering of the last sovereign, Alfonso XIII, was counted from the King of the Asturias, Alfonso I, who died as far back as 757; the succession being taken through Castile, Leon, Oviedo and Asturias.

The eldest son of the reigning English sovereign becomes, either from birth or from the time of his parent's accession, Duke of Cornwall. The title of Prince of Wales must, however, be conferred by the sovereign. There have been twenty-one Princes of Wales, from Edward of Caernarvon, later the unfortunate King Edward II, to the present Prince Charles. What is the origin of this title? John Selden remarks (*Titles of Honour*, Second Part, ch v): 'Whence the title of Prince of Wales was first transferred to the sons and heirs apparent of England is well enough known, but not so clearly when it began in them. It was transferred from those Princes of Wales (of North Wales especially) that in the elder times being Welsh, held the country under the Kings of England, by the name

99

of Princes. Neither was there any other besides them to whom the peculiar title of Prince was attributed, as it is a subordinate dignity. *Princeps Walliae*, and *Dominus Snowdoniae*, was their usual title.'

Who were these native Princes of Wales? The terms 'Welsh' and 'Wales' derive from an outlook which may be called typically English. The cultured English ruler of the nineteenth or early twentieth century, who could speak of himself as alone when surrounded by hundreds of natives, might think that he had little in common with the fierce tribesmen from western Germany who overturned Roman Britain. They, however, had no time for natives. The Britons were to the invading Saxons just foreigners, 'weallas', strangers in the land of their birth and the name has stuck despite all the manifestations of a resurgent Cymry. After 250 years of struggle the English kingdoms were established on the ruins of the old province of Britain. The Welsh were pent up in mountainous areas or regions difficult of access, Wales itself, Cumberland, Strathclyde and Cornwall, all destined to be subjugated by the accursed Saxon or his successors, and all doomed, except Welsh Wales, to have their language obliterated by English. The great King of Mercia, Offa *(Rex totius Anglorum patriae)*, who reigned from 757 to 796, built a dyke which still preserves his name to prevent Welsh trespassing upon Mercia. Thereafter the English attempted no conquest of Wales, though Harold, when Earl of Wessex, devastated Wales and brought the Welsh prince Gruffyd to his death. When William I succeeded Harold, he lost no time in exacting homage from the Welsh princes. Moreover, he encouraged his barons to attack Wales. By 1100, large parts of southern Wales were under Norman control. For a long time relations between Welsh prince and English king remained unsettled, brief periods of freedom for the Welsh being punctuated by longer spells when enmity erupted into disastrous war. At last Edward I conquered Wales, organised it in counties, but left Welsh law remaining. It was the task of Henry VIII, a Welshman on his father's side, to substitute English law for Welsh custom, and to form the union of England and Wales, still subsisting.

When Edward I was conquering Wales, his main objective midway in the campaign was to hold what he had won. He brought his pregnant Queen to Caernarvon Castle, so that she might give birth to their child in Wales. The old story was that Edward presented his new-born son to the Welsh chieftains when they asked for a prince of their own, with the saying that they should have for prince one who could not speak a word of English. This may be true and Edward may have early intended to make his son Prince of Wales. The future Edward II received a grant of the Principality of Wales and the County of Chester on 7 February 1301. He was summoned to Parliament as Prince of Wales and Earl of Chester on 2 June 1302.

From that time to the present, the eldest son of the reigning sovereign has borne the title of Prince of Wales. In two cases where the Prince has died before succeeding to the throne, his own son (grandson of the reigning monarch) has been created Prince. Definite creation there must be, and it depends entirely upon the will of the sovereign. The investiture of a Prince is altogether distinct from the act and time of creation of his title.

A Prince of Wales has other titles. The full list of the present holder is : H.R.H. Prince Charles Philip Arthur George, Prince of Wales and Earl of Chester, Duke of Cornwall in the Peerage of England, Duke of Rothesay, Earl of Carrick, and Baron of Renfrew in the Peerage of Scotland, Lord of the Isles and Great Steward of Scotland.

The title of Duke of Cornwall dates from a charter of 1337, by which Edward III made his eldest son, then Earl of Chester and the famous Black Prince, Duke of Cornwall. This was the first occasion of the title of a dukedom in England. Under the terms of the charter, the eldest son of the sovereign becomes from birth, or from the accession of the parent, Duke of Cornwall.

At the two kingdoms of England and Scotland are united, the Prince is heir to both and thus bears the titles in the Peerage of Scotland which were borne by the heir to the Scottish throne. On this Selden (Second Part, ch vii) remarks, 'The prince and heir apparent there (ie, in Scotland) they style the Prince of Scotland, and the rest of the King's children they call also princes as in other nations. The Prince of Scotland is as Prince, Duke of Rothesay, and High Steward of Scotland. And this Duchy of Rothesay was also the first Duchy there.' The title of Great Steward comes from the Stuart ancestor of the royal house who was High Steward of Scotland. Walter, the sixth High Steward, married Marjorie, daughter of King Robert the Bruce, and their son eventually became king as Robert II, and was ancestor of the royal line of Stuart.

Lord of the Isles, beautiful and romantic in sound, was once a harsh menace to the peace of Scotland. In the middle ages, the head

101

of Clan Donald was the Lord of the Isles, those lying off the western coast. In 1354 John, son of Angus Og, assumed the title of *Dominus Insularum*. He and other Lords of the Isles scarcely condescended to recognise the King of Scots as their liege lord, and when they felt sufficiently strong, they behaved as independent princes. The Lordship of the Isles lasted until 1493; the last holder of the title had made a treaty with Edward IV of England, as one sovereign with another. By its terms, Scotland was to be divided between the Lord of the Isles, the Earl of Douglas, and the King of England. When the treaty became known to the Scots king, he forced the Lord of the Isles to give up some of his lands to the Crown and to hold as from the Crown his originally self-appointed title. This was in 1476, and when further trouble occurred in 1493 the title was forfeited to the Crown, and later borne by the heir to the throne.

What of times antecedent to the creation of either Princedom or Dukedom of Cornwall? In the days of the Old English Kings, the heir apparent was styled *Clito*, and the other sons, *Clitones* or *Clitunculi*. This title is supposed to have come from the ancient Greek Κλύτος meaning 'famous, renowned, glorious' and hence 'noble'. As the English rulers had taken βασιλεύς for themselves, it was not unnatural for their sons to be styled Κλύτος. The term 'Atheling' was frequently employed for the heir to the throne, as in the case of the prince, Edgar Atheling who, after Hastings, was elected King, but who never reigned and had within a few weeks the ignominious task of tendering his crown to the Conqueror. This title was almost equivalent to *nobilis*, as can be seen in some of King Alfred's renderings from Bede's *Ecclesiastical History*. It came to be restricted to the person who looked as if he would succeed to the throne, bearing in mind that election played a large part in determining succession in those days. Thus William, son of Henry I, was termed the Atheling. Presumably he would have succeeded his father had he not been drowned when the *White Ship* went down.

The earldom of Chester was a County Palatine and as such was possessed by various powerful nobles until the death of the last of these in 1237, John le Scot, Earl of Huntingdon, nephew of William the Lion, King of Scotland. It was then annexed to the Crown and in 1254 it was granted to Prince Edward, the son and heir of Henry III. When this prince became King Edward I, the earldom merged in the Crown. An Act of Richard II (1398) ruled that the earldom was always to belong to the eldest son of the

102

sovereign. Henry IV repealed this Act but the earldom has never been granted since then except in conjunction with the Principality of Wales. Through his peerages, the Prince of Wales has the right to a seat in the House of Lords.

The distinction of Prince of Wales is purely titular and carries with it no power or responsibility. There have been times, as with the future Edward VII, when the sovereign rigorously excluded the Prince from knowledge of state papers. By the foundation statutes of the Order of the Garter, the Prince of Wales on his creation automatically becomes Knight of the Garter, but does not take his place among the knights until he is of an age suitable for investiture.

The title of Prince Consort was bestowed by Queen Victoria upon her husband, Prince Albert of Saxe Coburg and Gotha, in 1857 by letters patent under the Great Seal. He did not become a British peer, although the Queen had wished for this, on her marriage to him in 1840. The Prince had borne the title of Most Serene Ducal Highness and on his naturalization was granted in lieu the style of His Royal Highness. He is the only person in British history to have borne the formal title of Prince Consort, though of our six Queens regnant,* five have had husbands. These were all consorts, but two of them (Philip and William, husbands respectively of Mary I and Mary II) were themselves sovereigns and could not therefore receive any accession of honour from a princely title. Queen Anne's husband, Prince George of Denmark, was made Duke of Cumberland and Knight of the Garter, but although a prince consort of a reigning queen did not receive the formal princely title.

Prince Philip was a prince of Greece and Denmark, but was naturalized a British subject on 28 February 1947, when he adopted the surname of Mountbatten and renounced his rights of succession to the thrones of Greece and Denmark. On 19 November 1947 he was created Knight of the Garter, and granted the style of His Royal Highness. On 20 November 1947 (his wedding day) he was created Baron Greenwich, Earl of Merioneth and Duke of Edinburgh. It was not then correct to style him Prince Philip (despite the H.R.H.), though the usage was almost always employed in the popular press, mainly because it made an easier headline, than the correct Duke of Edinburgh. At length, on 22 February 1957, the Duke was granted

* The six Queens were Mary I, Elizabeth I, Mary II, Anne, Victoria, Elizabeth II, but really Matilda and Lady Jane Grey (Queen for nine days) should be included.

by the Queen the style and titular dignity of Prince of the United Kingdom.

The titles of members of the British royal house are governed by letters patent of 30 November 1917, by which King George V ruled that the titular dignity of Prince and Princess should for the future be restricted to children of the sovereign, the children of the sons of any such sovereign, and the eldest son of the eldest son of the Prince of Wales. These persons have the right to the style of Royal Highness. The title of Prince or Princess is prefixed to the respective Christian name. By the same letters patent the King ruled that all titles of Royal Highness not borne under the above terms, and all titles of Highness or Serene Highness, should cease to be borne, except in the case of those titles already granted and remaining unrevoked. These changes were made pursuant to a proclamation in which the King declared that the name of Windsor should be borne by his royal house, and that the use of all German titles and dignities in the royal family should cease. The family name was thus settled, and it is clear that the Germanic ancestry of the royal family had no surname, because, as Sir Bernard Burke remarked, they were of such ancient stem that the practice of taking surnames did not then exist. The royal houses of Stuart and Tudor had surnames because they had come to their greatness at a time when surnames were being taken; the Stuarts as we know were literally Stewards at one time, and the Tudors evidently tenant farmers, the surname being originally a Christian name. The Saxon and Norman houses had no surname, and that of Plantaganet was bestowed much later.

Previous to 1917 the style of princes and princesses of our royal family was governed by letters patent of Queen Victoria of 30 January 1864, by which the grandsons of the sovereign in the male and female line were granted the style of H.R.H. Before this date the descendants in the male line were H.H. only, except the sons and daughters of the sovereign, who were H.R.H.

After the 1917 ruling it is clear that some of the descendants of Queen Victoria, eg, Princess Marie Louise, one of the Queen's granddaughters, bore the style of H.H., while the children of the sovereign and the grandchildren who were born to the sovereign's sons were H.R.H.

Among many Scots there has been a picturesque revival of Jacobitism. Those who remember Sir Walter Scott's novels, *Waverley* and *Redgauntlet,* and who are English in birth and upbringing, have

104

probably assumed almost unconsciously that the Jacobite cause died in 1745-46 after the romantic episode of Prince Charles Edward's attempt to regain the crown for the Stuarts. However, today many writers of Scots birth and outlook can be found who refer to the army which won Culloden as the Hanoverian Army, even when they themselves hold commissions in the British Army, the same force as that called by them Hanoverian in 1746. They also refer to the person whom most of us call the Old Pretender as James VIII. I do not know if any call the Cardinal York, Henry IX, but I should not be surprised to find this so. How then do these writers manage to be loyal to the present dynasty (descended from the Hanoverians), and to hold commissions in its armed forces? The answer lies in one of those ingenious theories which are so helpful to poor mortals bemused by the bludgeonings of fate. In older times there was a principle of tanistry known among the Irish clans, and hence among the Scots, under which the successor to the chief was recognised during his lifetime and who need not be the direct lineal heir but must belong to the same family as the chief. In fact, this theory was found in the Old English kingdom where there was, as we have seen, a very real election to the throne but from among the royal house. Alfred the Great was preferred to the children of his elder brother because he was adult at the time when a new king was needed. The descendants of this branch of the English royalty lived on without any attempt at the throne. Probably one of the reasons for Harold's failure to keep the throne in 1066 lay in the fact that he was not of the royal family, an Atheling born. Had he possessed the cunning to make Edgar Atheling King, with himself as the power behind the throne, he could have quite probably beaten William the Conqueror at his own shifty legalistic game.

Accepting the principle of tanistry (the word comes from Irish *tanaiste*, heir to prince and *tan*=territory), the new Jacobites have become fervent loyalists to the present sovereign without losing their Stuart loyalties. The last male heir of the Stuarts was Henry Benedict Stuart, younger brother of the Young Pretender, Bonnie Prince Charlie, who died in 1788. Following him, Henry, who was a cardinal of the Church of Rome, with the title of Cardinal York, assumed the title of Henry IX, but made no attempt whatever to push his claims. In fact, he had a medal struck bearing the words (concerning his royal title) *Voluntate Dei, non hominum* : By the will of God, but not of men. He lived quietly at Rome on a pension

105

granted by George III, and when he died in 1807 he left some of his jewels to the King, which later passed to George IV. The monument in St Peter's, Rome, to the Old Pretender, the Young Pretender and the Cardinal was erected at the expense of the British sovereign. Thus to all true Jacobites George IV was the tanastair, lawful heir to the Stuarts and hence to be given the same loyalty. Little wonder that George IV after his accession was the first sovereign of the House of Hanover to visit Scotland, where he was received with enthusiasm, and actually wore the royal Stuart tartan. His visit was stage-managed by Sir Walter Scott.

10. The British Titled System

The British titled system is unique. It is true that there are a few countries in which titles are recognised by the State, but there is not another country in which they are still granted by the Crown. Partly, this is due to the considerable decrease in the number of monarchies in the present century. The great empires of Russia, Germany, Austria, Turkey and China have changed from monarchies to republics, and the kingdoms which remain, such as the Scandinavian royalties, no longer grant titles to their subjects, in deference to the strength of Socialist opinion. In Sweden, the House of Nobles, formerly comparable in function with our House of Lords, is no longer part of the Swedish constitution, having been replaced in the nineteenth century by a Second Chamber, which is elected not hereditary. The building itself is an interesting historical relic which contains illustrations of the arms of noble families and is a centre of attraction for the historically-minded tourists. The last Swede to be created a nobleman was the famous Central Asian explorer, Sven Hedin, in 1903. Grants of arms in Sweden are now largely a matter for bodies public, townships and the like. (See note at end of chapter.)

By a curious contrast, two of the republics which have seceded from the well-nigh vanished British Empire, Ireland and South Africa, have set up State Heralds. Even so, it is not the function of these officials to grant titles.

Even within the territories which still recognise Elizabeth II as Queen—Canada, Australia and New Zealand—it is now agreed that the Queen does not bestow titles on the citizens of most of those countries. The creation of titles is really confined to the United Kingdom of Great Britain and Northern Ireland, though even here the progress of Socialist opinion during the last few years has been such that hereditary titles have ceased to be created. Life peerages are now the rule, though they have to conform to the style of hereditary peerages, eg, every peerage title must have a territorial flavour in its letters patent. Baronetcies are never created. Under the Labour Government of 1945-51 there were no new baronetcies except for those conferred on the retiring Lord Mayors of London, a tradition which the Wilson administration has felt strong enough to break. If the Socialists should now achieve as long a period in office as their Conservative predecessors, thirteen years will surely establish a custom too strong to allow for the revival of hereditary peerages.

The British titled system is, therefore, in process of ossification. It is not likely to disappear as long as Left-wing leaders wish to join one of the best clubs in the world, and as long as women like being addressed as 'My Lady'. Portions of the system are already fossilized. Not since 1874 has anyone been made a duke unless he were either of royal birth or allied in marriage to royalty. No marquesses have been created since 1936, and life peerages are now limited to baronies. The guerdon of a retiring prime minister is an earldom. Will Earl Wilson be the first life recipient of the third penny?*

To describe the British titles is then to deal for the most part with purely historical matters. Not entirely so, however, for there are still many hundreds of peers whose titles are hereditary. Every year sees the publication of the *Roll of the Lords Spiritual and Temporal*, and the latest issue, dated 30 October 1968, published by Her Majesty's Stationery Office to sell at 6s 6d, contains 1,098 entries, of which about 900 were for hereditary peers. In addition, there are about seventy Irish peers who are still, after the reforms introduced by the Peerage Act of 1963, excluded from the Roll. Thus it can easily be realized that hereditary peerages are still very much an integral part of the British way of life.

The grades of the peerage in ascending order are : baron, viscount, earl, marquess and duke. Within each of these grades there are five sub-sections, which have arisen from historical causes. Eg, the barons are divided into the following classes : those of England, of Scotland, of Great Britain, of Ireland, and of the United Kingdom and of Ireland since the Union (1801). The historical background of these divisions is the story of the unification of England, Scotland and Ireland. The crowns of England and Scotland were united in 1603; there were then two distinct peerages of the two countries. When the Scottish Parliament was united with that of England in

---

* In feudal times an earl was entitled to a third penny, ie, a third of the revenues from the county court.

1707, there was henceforth a new division of the peerage, that of Great Britain. The older titles of the English and the Scottish peerages remained, but peerages created after 1707 were of Great Britain. No new creations took place in the English or Scottish peerages. A peerage which was dormant or in abeyance in those two older divisions could be revived, and though this has taken place no new titles have been made. Meanwhile, a separate peerage of Ireland continued, and a separate Irish legislation until 1801, when it was united with the Parliament of Great Britain. Since that date nearly all peerages have been of the United Kingdom. Not all Scottish or Irish peers were automatically entitled to sit in the House of Lords. Scottish peers were able, under the Treaty of Union, to elect sixteen of their number to sit in the House in each Parliament. The other unelected Scots peers did not sit in the Lords, unless they also possessed a peerage of Great Britain or (later) of the United Kingdom.

Irish peers after 1801 were able to elect twenty-eight of their own body to represent them in the Lords. These sat for life, and when the Irish Free State (now the Republic of Ireland) was established in 1921, no more elections of Irish peers took place. The last Irish representative peer, the Earl of Kilmorey, died in 1961. Irish, like Scots peers, were often members of the House in virtue of a peerage of Great Britain or of the United Kingdom. To complicate matters even more, a Scots or Irish peer sitting in right of his other peerage was listed by the latter title which was often of a lower rank, but in the House he would be addressed or referred to by his higher rank. Irish peers who were not elected to the Lords were permitted to stand for election to the House of Commons. The famous instance is that of the late Earl Winterton who was an M.P. for forty-seven years and Father of the House of Commons; yet when he retired from the Lower House he was promoted two degrees downward as Baron Turnour in the peerage of the United Kingdom to enable him to sit in the Lords. Scottish peers did not enjoy the opportunity of election to the Commons, but their anomalous position was put right by the Peerage Act of 1963, by which all Scots peers are now entitled to be members of the Lords. Irish peers unblessed with a U.K. peerage remain in the wilderness.

The first title in the peerage, in ascending order, that of baron (the King's man), was applicable to the great tenants (tenants *in capite*) of the Crown. Before there existed any Parliament in the same

109

sense in which the term has been understood for the past 700 years, there was a Great Council of the notables of the realm, ecclesiastical as well as lay. Under the Old English kings, the Council was called the Witenagemot, or meeting of the wise, usually abbreviated to Witan. The Norman kings carried on this institution and to it came (in the words of the *Anglo-Saxon Chronicle*), 'all the men of England . . . archbishops, bishops, and abbots, earls, thegns, and knights'. The occasions for the summoning of the Council were those solemn festivals of the Christian year : 'Thrice a year King William (the Conqueror) wore his crown every year he was in England; at Easter he wore it at Winchester, at Pentecost at Westminster and at Christmas at Gloucester', says the *Chronicle* (quoted in F. W. Maitland's *Constitutional History of England*, 1908, p 61.)

The ecclesiastical lords had been important in England from the days of its conversion to Christianity. Apart from their position as church leaders, they also had temporal responsibilities for they were landowners in virtue of their sees and monasteries. The lay lords were the remaining great tenants of the Crown, and they came to be known as the barons, a term not used in England before the Conquest. The greater barons were those who received a summons to the Great Council, the *Magnum Concilium* into which the Witan developed and from which the Privy Council evolved. In course of time English lawyers worked out a theory according to which a person who received a summons to the Council was a peer, and his son inherited his peerage. The facts of history are in contradiction of this theory.

Slowly and over a long period, a peerage system was evolved, and it was perhaps unfortunate that, in the process, the word 'baron' should have been used both in the feudal and in a more modern meaning. As to the term *baro*, Maitland's remarks are very apposite : 'It would seem that at this time (ie, twelfth century), the title baron covered all the military tenants in chief of the Crown. This is in accordance with the original meaning of the word—*baro* is simply man; this meaning it long kept in our law French : husband and wife are baron and *feme*; but man is the term opposed to lord; the man does homage to his lord, *hominium* or *homagium*, from *homo* a man; and it seems somewhat of an accident that while we speak of the homage of a manorial court, meaning thereby the body of tenants owing suit and service, we speak of the baronage of the king's courts; the king's tenants-in-chief are his *hommes* and his

110

barones also.' (*op cit* p 65.) In a recent work, *English Baronies, A Study of Their Origin and Descent*, 1086-1327, Mr I. J. Sanders has made it entirely clear that the older baronies had no necessary relationship with our modern conception of peerage, ie, the legal theory paramount over the past 400 years. The author states that the most searching test as to baronial status was the payment of baronial relief. The mere use of such language takes us at once into a feudal world where the lawyer's definition of peerage is quite out of place. The feudal baron was not what the Tudor lawyers called a lord; he was the holder of land as a chief tenant of the Crown. This feudal concept of lordship has departed completely from English legal theory, but still exists in Scotland where a considerable distinction is made between a minor baron, who is a laird and the holder of a medieval barony, and a 'Lord of Parliament'. The English peerage evolved over centuries out of a feudal baronage. As to what constituted a *baro major*, we may be content to acquiesce with Maitland in practical ignorance.

The barons of the middle ages were a class, the name was generic, and included earls within it. The baron created by letters patent is a peer, the possessor of the lowest rank in the peerage. Today, and for the past 500 years, all peerages, with very rare exceptions, are created by letters patent. A very unusual instance to the contrary occurred in 1951 when the present 3rd Earl of Ancaster was summoned to the House of Lords by writ in one of his father's baronies as Lord Willoughby de Eresby. The object of this proceeding was to enable him to discharge his father's duties as Lord Great Chamberlain, the latter being in ill health at the time. Our oldest peerages have been held to be created by writ of summons to the Lords (that is to the Great Council which existed before Parliament began). A relic of this mode of creation is found in the usage of issuing writs to peers to attend Parliament. There have been other methods of creation, as by charter which may be taken to be a form of letters patent; also at one time by tenure. The only reminder of this last method is the sometimes quoted legend that the ownership of Arundel Castle bears with it a peerage, so that the possessor of the property would become Earl of Arundel. It is settled law that there is no such thing as a peerage by tenure in England.

It was not until the fourteenth century that the House of Lords as such could be rightly distinguished from the Great Council, and it was not until 1387 that a peerage was made which was purely a personal honour and quite unconnected with offices known to the feudal system. This was the barony granted by Richard II to John Beauchamp, as Baron Beauchamp of Kidderminster. The style given to a baron is the Right Honourable the Lord X, and they are officially addressed by the Crown as 'Right trusty and well beloved'. The use of the form, 'Right Honourable' derives from the days long past when nearly all peers were members of the Privy Council. Privy Councillors were always addressed as Right Honourable. From this custom it came that all peers of the rank of earls, viscounts and barons are styled Right Honourable, and in this way a courteous social usage grew up. The habit of addressing these three ranks in the peerage as Right Honourable went without challenge until some years back when an attempt was made to restrict it to the minority of peers who were also Privy Councillors. This idea was abandoned when it was confirmed that 'Right Honourable' was correct for all peers below the rank of marquess.

So much for the origin and history of the title of baron. It can be said in passing that, in Continental usage, it is correct to refer to Baron X, but quite wrong in the case of a British baron. 'Baron' is never used of a British lord, save in very formal language. The title 'Lord' is taken from the Old English *hlaford*, a combination of *hlafa*—loaf—(cf. Lammas or Loaf Mass), and *weard* or warder. The feminine form, *Lady*, is from *hlafdige*, a loaf kneader. The Saxon lord and lady were thus the providers of bread to their dependents. Nothing could eradicate this term, no matter how much the Norman seigneurs tried. Even the Countess (a title which won its way where Count failed) is addressed as 'Lady'.

The old English title for a nobleman was *ealdorman* or alderman, older or senior man. Thus we have the hero Brythnoth, immortalised in the Old English poem, *The Battle of Maldon*, who as *Ealdorman* of East Anglia rallies the English forces against the Danes. When Alfred the Great's daughter, Ethelfleda, married the sub-king of Mercia, he then bore the title of *Ealdorman*; he had previously been known as King, but on accepting Alfred's rulership he took the lesser but still noble title. About a century before the Conquest the title of earl—an English translation of *jarl*, the term used to describe the Viking leaders—began to be used for the greater English noblemen. Thereafter alderman was a title which became restricted to lesser dignitaries and so gradually descended to our civic functionaries.

112

The earl of pre-Conquest days was a ruler under the King of a large areas such as Northumberland, Mercia, Wessex, East Anglia or Sussex. These titles were *ex officio*, not by any means inheritable, and were often resumed by the Crown. The reign of Edward the Confessor (1042-66) is very much the story of the rivalry of the houses of Leofric and of Godwin. After the Norman Conquest the position of an earl, though still that of an office, was becoming much more a title of honour. In each county there was the Shire Reeve, or Sheriff, an official appointed by the King and removable by him. The title of earl soon became hereditary : under King Stephen, Geoffrey de Mandeville was created Earl of Essex with inheritance by his heirs. This person, one of the most reprehensible in the Anarchy, was created earl by Stephen's rival, Matilda, as his influence was sought by both sides in the struggle. In 1328 the Earldom of March was made without any pretence at territorial connection. For a long time now titles such as that of Earl Attlee, where the title accompanies the surname, have been common. The term 'belted earl' refers to the girding of a newly-made earl with a sword, a ceremony discontinued after the time of Edward VI.

The title of viscount has been mentioned as that of a *vice-comes*. It was used as a title of nobility when Henry VI created John, Lord Beaumont, in 1440, Viscount Beaumont. When officially addressed by the Crown he is styled 'Right trusty and well beloved cousin', the style also used for earls. The great jurist, Blackstone, assigns the use of the word 'cousin' to Henry IV who, being related to all the higher ranks of the peerage, 'artfully and constantly acknowledged that connection in all his letters and other public acts; whence the usage has descended to his successors, though the reason has long ago failed.'

The marquess's title began in England in 1385 when Richard II created Robert de Vere, his favourite, Marquess of Dublin. In 1397 John Beaufort, Earl of Somerset, became Marquess of Dorset. The style of address of a marquess is 'Most Honourable'. He, too, is addressed formally by the Crown as 'Our Right Trusty and entirely beloved Cousin'. Marquesses also on certain formal occasions are given the title of 'Most Noble and Puissant Prince', in line with the usage of addressing great Continental nobles as Prince, eg, in Poland. An English duke has, if he wishes, the style of 'Most High, Potent and Noble Prince'.

In view of the prevalence of the ducal title in continental Europe, it may seem strange that no dukes were created in England until 1337, when King Edward III made the Black Prince Duke of Cornwall. This title, as we have mentioned earlier, is a special creation by charter, with peculiar provisions. In 1351, a Duke of Lancaster was created but the recipient died in 1361 issueless and Edward III's younger son, John of Gaunt, was then made Duke of Lancaster. This title merged in the Crown when Gaunt's son, Henry, became Henry IV. As the dukedom of Lancaster still exists, as it were *in gremio regis*, the sovereign, whether king or queen, is referred to in Lancashire by Lancastrians as Duke of Lancaster. By both George VI and Elizabeth II this title has been accepted when in Lancashire, let pedants disguise their boring disloyalty as they please. In passing, it can be stated that there is no title of Duke of Normandy as applied to British sovereigns. King John lost possession of Normandy in 1204 and by a treaty in 1259 between France and England the title of Duke of Normandy was renounced by the English king. The Channel Islands are territorially part of the old Normandy, but sovereignty over them was reserved to the English Crown. An echo of old controversies was heard at the International Court at the Hague in 1953 when the French claimed the sovereignty over some rocks known as Les Ecrehous and Les Minquiers, near Jersey. British sovereignty over the latter was affirmed by the court, which listened to arguments based on centuries-old treaties and documents.

The English kings were for 300 years Dukes of Aquitaine, but this title was lost when the English dominion in France ended in 1453. For several centuries in the coronation of English sovereigns two lay figures represented the Duke of Aquitaine and the Duke of Normandy. At the coronation of Queen Anne 'it was remembered that the high offices of the Dukes of Normandy and Aquitaine were represented by Jonathan Andrews and James Clark' (Dean Stanley, *Historical Memorials of Westminster Abbey*, 1868, p 97) and at the coronation of George III in 1761, 'The English representatives of the Dukes of Aquitaine and Normandy appeared for the last time, and with them the last relics of our dominion over France vanished.' (Stanley, *ibidem*, p 104, who adds in a footnote that these lay figures took precedence over the Archbishop of Canterbury.) The reason for their non-appearance at later coronations was that George III in 1800 renounced the title of King of France and ceased to quarter the fleurs-de-lis in his royal shield.

The number of dukedoms has never been great. For some thirty years (1572-1603) there were no dukes in England. Even now there are only twenty-seven, plus five royal dukes, Gloucester, Kent, Windsor, Edinburgh, and Cornwall. The style of a duke is 'His Grace'.

In English peerage law even the heir to a peerage is a commoner, only the reigning peer and his wife being classed as noble. Consequently any titles borne or used by peers' children are entirely matters of courtesy. The eldest son of a duke, marquess, or earl will use one of the father's subsidiary titles. The latter arise from the fact that most of the higher have been promoted from the lower ranks of the nobility. Even when a commoner is made an earl he will usually have a secondary title, eg, the 1st Earl Attlee was also Viscount Walthamstow, by which title his son was known. This practice has given rise to immense difficulties for those who are ignorant of the technicalities of the British peerage. The eldest son of a peer is eligible during his father's lifetime to become an M.P., and the House of Commons usually contains a sprinkling of marquesses, earls and viscounts who are not peers.

The grandsons of the dukes and marquesses often bear yet another of the grandfather's subsidiary titles. Younger sons of dukes are known as, eg, Lord Randolph Churchill, father of Sir Winston Churchill. A duke's daughter is Lady Mary Smith. A marquess's younger sons and his daughters are styled in the same way as for ducal offspring, and this also applies to an earl's daughters. The women keep this style on marriage, except that the husband's surname is substituted for the paternal. A courtesy usage has rarely been understood, with the result that newspaper reports abound with inaccurate references to knights' and baronets' wives as Lady Mary etc, as though they were daughters of earls.

An earl's younger son is called the Honourable Edward X. The sons and daughters of viscounts and barons are similarly styled and the women retain the title of 'Honourable' after their marriage, unless married to peers.

A life peer is as much noble as an hereditary peer. His style is identical and his wife and children have the same styles as those of the hereditary nobles. A woman who is a peeress in her own right and who is married is usually addressed as eg, The Countess of Seafield (Mrs Studley Herbert).

Baronets are a unique feature of a unique system. They date as an order from 1611 when James I instituted the title so that he might raise money. The title of baronet was known before his time, but considerable ambiguity exists as to its medieval meaning. There are thirteen instances of the use of the word between 1307 and 1603, and in one case, when Edward III created a baronet, the title was hereditary. There has been confusion between a banneret and a baronet, and it is possible that the latter is derived from the former. A medieval knight banneret was a knight entitled to lead a company of vassals under his banner. A knight bore a pennon, which was a forked swallow-tail flag of the kind seen in many medieval pictures. A banner, on the contrary, was square, and it is said that an especially valorous knight would have his pennon cut, removing the forked ends and leaving a diminutive banner. The banneret had precedence over other knights.

A baronetcy is hereditary. There are some 1,500 baronets, and of these about 250 are also peers. There are five classes and these, with the dates of creation, are: of England (1611), Ireland (1611), Scotland or Nova Scotia (1625), Great Britain (1707), and of the United Kingdom (1801).

The style of a baronet is Sir John Smith, and in any writing, the word 'Baronet' should be added, either in full, or more commonly as 'Bart.' The official abbreviation, approved by the Standing Council of the Baronetage (a species of trade union, designed to protect the order) is Bt, which suffers from the fact that it cannot be pronounced whereas 'Bart' is easily said and familarly known. The wife of a baronet is styled Lady Smith.

The order of knights has undergone a long evolution from its origin as the backbone of medieval warfare. Today, there are eleven orders of chivalry—although four are obsolescent—which give to their recipients the right to put the title 'Sir' before their names. In addition to these there is the original knightly order, now known as that of knight bachelor. The origin of the title is variously assigned; some think it a corruption of *battalier*, or fighter on the battlefield. In the scale of precedence the order of knight bachelor comes after all the orders of chivalry which have been developed from it. Yet the knight bachelor is the real representative of the fighting knights of the middle ages, for from the main body of knights the various chivalric orders have been hived off. This is true of all Western European countries. In England, the Order of the Garter dates from 1348, but obviously there were very many knights before that time.

116

The origin of the title of knight in England is said to be the Old English *cnicht*, a boy or attendant, an explanation which may not seem very honourable when, in modern parlance, the word 'boy' is so often used of persons who are anything but boyish, and certainly not good boys; eg, robbers, murderers, gangsters and hooligans. Our ancestors of the Conquest period saw the arrival in their country of some very rough characters, the followers of William the Conqueror, to whom he gave the lands of England. In other countries the equivalent name to the English 'knight' referred to the fact that he was a mounted man. Thus, in France, *chevalier*, in Spain, *caballero*, and in Germany *ritter*. We can even go back to the Roman *eques*, denoting a member of the order of knights who ranked below the senatorial class. The Roman name was originally given to persons who supplied the Roman cavalry, though this soon ceased to be true. The Roman *miles*, or soldier, perhaps corresponds most nearly to the medieval knight, but the chivalric character of the latter was entirely absent from the former.

Some ancient writers, such as Tacitus in his *Germania*, can be pressed into service to show that there was a ceremony of arms-bestowing among the Germanic tribes. Probably there was something of the nature of giving the tomahawk among the Red Indians, and wherever a young warrior was initiated into the warrior band, but this is not admittance to a chivalric order. In the middle ages, the Christian Church endeavoured to build a Christian civilisation on the ruins of paganism. She took the arms-giving ritual, gave it a distinctive character surrounded with religious sanctions, and with it sought to instil into the knightly aspirant a character higher than that of a mere warrior. Courtesy, gentleness towards the weak, piety and charity towards all, were inculcated. No doubt many knights failed to live up to the ideal but, nonetheless, there were many chivalrous lives. True, the Black Prince, the flower of English chivalry, ordered a general massacre at Limoges, but he did stop that massacre when he saw the brave resistance of some French knights, and he could certainly be a generous victor. The worst fault of the medieval knight probably lay in his inability to show kindness or mercy to those outside his own class. Over the years, a great literature grew up to suit the tastes of the warriors, principal among the romances being those of the Arthurian cycle.

An institution of dubbing a knight probably existed before the Norman Conquest in England, for there are instances of the in-

117

vestiture of a prince with mantle and sword. It is certainly true that in the earlier middle ages ecclesiastics often bestowed a knighthood, and the story in Kingsley's romance of Hereward being dubbed knight by his uncle, Abbot Brand, is in line with historical instances. Others beside the sovereign made knights and it was only by degrees that bestowal of the honour came to be the exclusive prerogative of the king or his deputy. The ceremony of making a knight, apart from the religious service in which it was enshrined, consisted, as it still does, in the touching of the shoulder of the new knight with a sword. The wife of a knight is styled Lady.

The chief orders of knighthood are :

(i) The Garter, instituted by Edward III after some of the great victories of his reign—Sluys, Crécy, Calais. Only persons of great distinction among his companions could be foundation knights of this order, and to this day a plain mister who is made a knight of the Garter, Thistle or other orders must be dubbed a knight bachelor before he can be invested with the insignia of the higher order. From early times there have been Ladies of the Garter, members of the royal house. There have also been additional knights in the person of foreign sovereigns.

(ii) The Thistle, which is the great order of Scotland and is supposed to have originated in the eighth century. Whatever the date of its creation, it was remodelled and given new statutes in 1687.

(iii) The Bath is formally dated from 1399, with new statutes in 1725. It probably represents the ancient ceremony by which those about to be knighted were wont to bathe themselves in token of purity. This was particularly the case at the coronation of a sovereign when a select number of new knights were made.

(iv) St Michael and St George was instituted in 1818 to reward natives of Malta and the Ionian Islands, the latter being then under the protection of Britain. The order is now used to reward British subjects who serve in foreign countries or are domiciled in British possessions overseas.

(v) The Royal Victorian order was instituted in 1896 for personal service to the Crown. The Garter and the Thistle have only one class. Of the other orders mentioned, the Bath and the St Michael and St George, also have a class of companions, while the Royal Victorian order has companions and members as well. GCVO denotes a Knight or Dame Grand Cross of the order.

(vi) The British Empire is an order instituted by George V in 1917. It has five classes, two of which (GBE and KBE) carry the title of Sir. Women are members of the order and those who are in either of the two highest classes are called Dame.

(vii) St Patrick was created in 1783 by George III. It was intended to honour notable Irish dignitaries. It ranked after the orders of the Garter and the Thistle. As late as 1924 the order was kept at its full strength of twenty-two, but today only the royal Dukes of Gloucester and Windsor remain to recall the past brilliance of this chivalric band. There are few more melancholy sights among the many melancholy relics of the former British Empire than that of the banners of the knights of St Patrick as they hang in the great hall of Dublin castle.

(viii) The Star of India was instituted by Queen Victoria in 1861. No appointments have been made since 1947.

(ix) The Indian Empire was instituted in 1886 and (x) The Crown of India, instituted in 1877, was designed for ladies. Both orders have been virtually defunct since 1947.

In addition to the above which, except for the Crown of India, carried titular distinctions, there are two orders which have a high rank but which do not confer a title. These are the order of Merit and the order of the Companions of Honour. The recipients of these may place the letters OM and CH after their names.

Apart from these titles, there are others which have an official rank in England. At the end of the Table of Precedence for England and that for Scotland occur two entries, esquires and gentlemen. There is an almost Egyptian darkness on the subject of the first of these in the minds of most people. When the present Lord Snowdon married Princess Margaret there was a very general impression both in England and on the Continent that the Princess had married a plebeian—'married beneath her' as it used to be described. This total misconception shows how far the British public had forgotten the real meaning of the title of 'esquire' which Mr Anthony Armstrong Jones gave as his rank in the marriage register. Esquire is as much a title as that of knight; it is granted from the sovereign and is inherited by the grantee's sons. About 1870 Queen Victoria granted the title of esquire to her faithful servant John Brown. When anyone obtains a grant of arms it carries with it the grant of the title of esquire. Thus the real test of nobility in the widest sense is the authentic possession of arms. Armigerous persons are gentle and they occupy the lowest rank in nobility. Sir Bernard Burke often wrote of the untitled aristocracy of Britain, and indeed his well-known *Peerage* had its essential companion volume in the *Landed Gentry*.

Except for the stumbling blocks of the few courtesy titles, members of peerage families are untitled. Even a duke's grandson is a simple mister, and the greatest Englishman of our time was content to pass most of his life as Mr Winston Churchill. It cannot seriously be contended by the most caste-ridden aristocrat of continental Europe that an English squire or a Scottish laird of gentle family is inferior in status to the *comtes* and *vicomtes* whom the debris of the European empires so liberally supply. Nobiliary status, the possession of arms, gives the rank of esquire and the status of gentleman. Although the exigencies of mail-order salesmanship have bestowed the title of esquire upon the entire adult male population of Great Britain, this is still incorrect. There are rules which govern the use of esquire. Esquires are (i) those created expressly as such, with a collar of SS and spurs of silver (the spurs of a knight are, or should be, golden). (ii) persons chosen esquires to the Prince's body. This latter class is now obsolete; the former is covered still by the formal use of the title in an arms grant. (iii) The sons of all peers, during the lives of their fathers; younger sons of peers after the deaths of their fathers; the eldest sons of the younger sons of peers and their eldest sons. This shows how very flimsy are the courtesy titles; a man cannot be described as the Honourable John Smith, Esq, and the rules governing the use of esquire are older than the custom of courtesy titles. (iv) The eldest sons of baronets and knights; in fact, all sons in these two categories. (v) Esquires of the Bath and the eldest sons of those esquires pursuant to the statutes of the order. (vi) Noblemen of other nations and minor barons (laird barons) of Scotland. The modern rule regarding the latter is that a laird is not referred to as esquire, but described as John Wemyss of Weymss, always omitting Mr or Esq, and the use of a comma after the surname. However it was not always so and an instance to hand is the description of the celebrated Abyssinian traveller, James Bruce of Kinnaird, Esq, as his name appears on the title page of his book of travels (Alan Moorhead, *The Blue Nile*, World Reprint edition, p 41.)

Besides these classes in which the title is either granted or inherited, several categories exist where a custom or prescriptive right has bestowed esquiredom. (vii) Barristers-at-law by their office or profession. (viii) Justices of the Peace, and mayors while in commission, or in office (in Scotland this applied to provosts only of royal burghs.) (ix) Persons who attend at the sovereign's coronation in some notable capacity or office of trust, or serving in some better class of post in the royal households. (x) Sheriffs of counties, and the most junior officers in the armed forces. (xi) Attorneys in colonies, where the departments of counsel and attorney are united.

Esquires were originally attendants on the person of a knight, whom they followed to war and to whom they rendered various services. They looked forward to attaining knighthood but gradually the esquires came to denote the first degree in gentry or nobility.

It is usually forgotten that Mr is also a title. In its full form it is now given only to a boy, eg, Master John Robinson, but in former times it was very much a usage of honour and denoted that the person so addressed was worthy of respect. The form—the Rev Mr Jones—which seems so strange now is a good example of the way in which Mr was used in conjunction with other titles.

Usage, of course, dictates most titles, and only a comparative few are the subject of written regulation. This applies particularly to the custom by which most married women are known as Mrs, which stands for Mistress and is obviously the feminine of Mister (Master). From long ages of use it is firmly entrenched in our lives, and those who object to titles might pause to reflect how uncouth and rude our social intercourse would be if all titles disappeared. For with the Lords and Sirs would logically go the Mr and Mrs. Few married women would support this reform, however democratic it might be made out to be.

In a society where titles are banned by law, substitutes for them will be found. How frequent among Continental and American *literati* is the appearance of 'Doctor', and how readily have some learned faculties assisted this growing crop of Drs. It is not quite clear why Law should have been selected as the erudite study most suited to supply honorary degrees, but such is overwhelmingly the case. Next in popularity for degrees *honoris causa* is Literature, for which there is more reason. Few honorary PhDs are granted; this doctorate is the reward of ever more minute scholarship. It can be justified on the ground that philosophy, the love of wisdom, is the science of thought, from which the various particular sciences have been sectioned off, and that no serious study is beyond its boun-

121

daries. The term 'Doctor' is medieval and best explained by H. G. Wells' sarcastic comment that a Bachelor of Arts knew much, a Master of Arts more, and a Doctor most.

The commonest use of Doctor as a title is of course for a member of the medical profession, the majority of whom are not entitled to its use at all, since they do not proceed to MD. But so prevalent is the titular use that, in general parlance, a doctor who is not a medical practitioner has to explain that his doctorate is non-medical.

An amusing usage in recent years has been the extension of the title 'Emeritus' from academic circles to spheres far removed from university life. As originally used it denoted a professor who had retired from teaching but who continued in the university. Now it is applied to vergers, organists and others, and seems likely to be applied to anyone who retires.

Referring to academic life, it may be noted that the heads of Oxford colleges have a variety of titles : Rector at Exeter College; President at Corpus Christi; Dean at Christ Church; at All Souls, Warden; at Balliol, Master; at Jesus, Principal, and at Oriel, Provost.

NOTE : Further to my references to the House of Nobles in Sweden, and other Swedish matters, a Swedish correspondent sends me the following note:

'The King is clad in uniform (a general's) with collars at the opening of the Riksdag; the royal robes (mantle) are laid on the throne; we have two honours lists including the royal orders of knighthood and medals; on 6 June (the National or Swedish Flag Day) and in connection with the King's birthday, 11 November;* the House of Nobles is still an official institution and the Noble Assembly is held every third year. In 1967 two new families ennobled in the seventeenth century were introduced. The State Herald is a First Archivist at the State Archives (Riksarkivet) and head of its heraldic section, where he has a (usually female) amanuensis—he has no uniform as such; for ceremonial (not heraldic) matters, Royal Majesty's Orders have a Herald of the Realm and two Heralds.'

I am glad to have this note at first hand, but still the House of Nobles, unlike the British House of Lords, is not any longer a part of the Swedish legislature. The introduction of two families ennobled in the seventeenth century into the Noble Assembly does not constitute the creation of nobility. It would correspond to the revival of a peerage in the English or Scottish peerage, which can indeed happen in Britain, although no new peerages are now created in those divisions of the British peerage.

* The correspondent means, of course, that these two dates are parallel to those of the British New Year and Birthday Honours Lists.

11. Monarchies of the Present Day

There remain still twenty-four monarchies in the world, using the term in the sense of a sovereign independent state whose government, headed by a monarch, not only manages its own internal affairs but also has control over its external policy. In practice, very few modern nations are completely independent in the sense that they proceed on a self-appointed course without regard to any other state. Among the great nations, possibly only Communist China can fulfil the requirements of the definition. There may still be places so remote from the centres of power, and so lacking in valuable products, that their poverty protects and secures their independence. Generally in the twentieth century, however, even the most powerful states find their independent sovereignty is qualified alike in external and internal affairs. Still, the definition is useful in this respect; there are a number of semi-sovereign states whose external direction lies with a suzerain, to employ an old but realistic word. The number has greatly diminished with the decolonisation of the European empires. The multiplication of separate national entities all claiming complete sovereignty renders the study of international politics one of thrilling uncertainty.

The existing twenty-four monarchies are distributed throughout Europe, Asia and Africa. In Europe they are : the United Kingdom; the Scandinavian states, Sweden, Norway and Denmark; Belgium, Holland, Greece, Monaco, Luxembourg and Liechtenstein. In Asia, there are Japan, Nepal, Bhutan, Thailand, Cambodia, Laos, Jordan, Persia (Iran), Saudi Arabia, Yemen, and Afghanistan. Africa provides only three : Libya, Morocco and Ethiopia.

In addition to these monarchies of independent states, there are scattered about the world a number of semi-sovereign royal houses which were once independent but which became dependent upon other, usually European, powers. Such thrones, if indeed they can

123

be so called, include the Sultanate of Bahrain, the Trucial Sheik-doms around the Persian Gulf, the monarch of Tonga, the Kabaka of Buganda, and various other formerly colonial chiefs. Among these relics, until 1946, could have been included the throne of the Rajahs of Sarawak, surely one of the most romantic dynasties in history. In 1839 Sarawak was part of the Malay Sultanate of Brunei, but there had been oppression and a revolt of the inhabitants. A young Englishman, James Brooke, arrived on the scene, coasting around in search of adventure, as did so many Englishmen in those times. He succeeded in settling the dispute and in return was given by the Sultan of Brunei the title and position of Rajah of Sarawak, under the Sultan. In 1845 the Sultan renounced his suzerainty and Rajah Brooke became an independent sovereign. There were three rajahs of the line, the last being Sir Charles Vyner Brooke who died in 1963 and who made over the state to the British Crown. The dynasty has its history traced in Burke's *Landed Gentry*, a family of crowned heads among the untitled aristocracy! The arms of the family are distinguished by the presence of that most unusual element in the arms of an untitled or non-peerage family, namely supporters, these being appropriately, a Malay man on the dexter side, and a Dyak woman on the sinister. The heir to the throne was called the Tuan Muda, and the daughters of the house were given names like Princess Gold etc, by the natives. When Charles Kingsley in 1855 brought out his novel, *Westward Ho!*, he dedicated the book to The Rajah Sir James Brooke, KCB, and George Augustus Selwyn, DD, Bishop of New Zealand (the latter was one of the martyrs of the Pacific area), with obviously profound respect.*

In a very different class were the Indian princes, 562 in number, who had nearly all been independent before the British ruled India. Among these were such outstanding potentates as His Exalted Highness, the Nizam of Hyderabad, whose country was larger than the area of several European states.

* The full dedication is as follows:
'By one who (unknown to them) has no other method of expressing his admiration and reverence for their characters. That type of English virtue at once manful and godly, practical and enthusiastic, prudent and self-sacrificing, which he has tried to depict in these pages, they have exhibited in a form even purer and more heroic than that in which he has drest it, and than that in which it was exhibited by the worthies whom Elizabeth, without distinction of rank or age, gathered round her in the ever glorious wars of her great reign.'

Among the semi-independent princes, only the King of Morocco has regained the status which his predecessors enjoyed before the French protectorate over Morocco. There is also the peculiar position of the Dalai Lama of Tibet, a ruler regarded by his subjects as a god on earth and now experiencing the rigours of exile known to so many other monarchs.

With these royal lines we are concerned in so far as they contribute titular distinctions. There has been in the present century so great an inroad upon the domains of monarchy that great changes have, in consequence, been made in the world of title.

The first people to challenge the divine right of kings were the English, but their dethronement of the Stuarts remained for 140 years without a following. Then, in the France of the French Revolution, the trial of Charles I became compulsive reading. The age of the tumbrils had begun, and the head of the French king fell at the behest of a fierce democracy, whereas Charles I had been beheaded by the orders of a masterful private gentleman who had as little sympathy with democracy as with Stuart absolutism. In the revolutionary era which followed the execution of Louis XVI thrones toppled all over Europe, but the hereditary monarchs were soon replaced by members of the Napoleonic family, just as Napoleon himself (within fifteen years of the death of the king) became self-appointed Emperor of the French. Only one Napoleonic monarchy survives, that of Bernadotte in Sweden, though this was founded, not by a Bonaparte but by one of his marshals. After Napoleon's disaster at Waterloo, 'kings crept out again', and most of the European monarchies regained their thrones. France never again became permanently royalist, and experienced numerous vicissitudes, including a republic whose president turned himself into an emperor. Napoleon III was never wholly recognised by some of the other European royalties (the Tzar did not accord him the salutation, *Mon Frère*, which he gave to his equals). The Second Empire and the Napoleonic dynasty succumbed in the debâcle of 1870.

The Spanish empire did not long survive the aftermath of the Napoleonic upheaval. The house of Braganza reigned in the empire of Brazil from 1808 until 1889, when royalty in the New World became confined to British territory. In Europe, the abolition of the Holy Roman Empire and the rise of the German Empire made serious inroads on independent regal sovereignty with the mediatisation of the Germanic princes. Even so, the twentieth century at its commencement was able to provide nine kings to ride in the funeral procession of Queen Victoria. The first country to lose its monarchy was Portugal, where King Manoel, head of the house of Braganza, succeeded in 1908 his father, Carlos I, who had been assassinated in Lisbon. King Manoel soon had to flee and a republic was proclaimed in 1910. He was the first sovereign to make the title of 'ex-king' well known in Europe. In 1912, the Son of Heaven, the Chinese Emperor, was forced to abdicate. The subsequent career of Henry Pu Yiu has been like a resumé of the political life of this century. A mere boy when he was driven from the Dragon Throne, the last of the Manchus was chosen puppet Emperor of Manchukuo (Manchuria) by the Japanese, dethroned again when Japan was defeated, then imprisoned and brain-washed by the followers of Mao Tse-tung, to end as a humble gardener in modern China, where he died in October 1967.

After the 1914-18 war, a wave of revolutions removed the imperial majesties of Austria-Hungary, Germany and Russia, the Sultan of Turkey, and the King of Montenegro, whose country was merged in Yugoslavia. In the period between the two world wars, one of the greatest of the old monarchies, that of the Bourbons of Spain, disappeared from the list of regal states. Alfonso XIII was the last King of Spain. Whether the Spanish monarchy will ever be restored is a query. The second world war brought with it the fall of several other monarchies, Italy, Bulgaria, Rumania, Yugoslavia and Albania all becoming republics. Thus within our century, twelve countries, six of them great powers, have turned from monarchy to republicanism.

Of the ten remaining European monarchies, seven—the United Kingdom, Sweden, Norway, Denmark, Belgium, Holland and Greece—have sovereigns who bear the title of His or Her (U.K. and Holland) Majesty the King or Queen. Two others, Monaco and Liechtenstein, have Princes who are denominated as Serene Highness. The tenth state, Luxembourg, is headed by a Grand Duchess, H.R.H. Three of these kingdoms—Norway, Denmark and Greece—possess sovereigns of the House of Schleswig-Holstein-Sonderboûrg-Glucksboûrg. To this family Prince Philip belongs and so, on naturalization, had to renounce his possible succession to the thrones of Denmark and Greece. The royal house of Holland is that of Orange Nassau; Luxembourg is ruled by the house of Nassau; Liechtenstein by a royal family of that name. The Grimaldis are the ruling family of Monaco.

Of the reigning royal families of Asia, easily the most interesting is that of Japan. The sovereign is His Majesty the Emperor, commonly known among Europeans as the Mikado—Honourable Gate. This title is not used by the Japanese themselves, except in poetry, and has been adopted by foreigners who have failed to grasp the true title of the Emperor. He is termed by his subjects the Tenno, or Tenshi, titles used to describe the Emperor precisely because they are not his real names. The true name of the god-king should not be breathed by the people, because it is so sacred. This belief has been widely held not only by the Japanese but in many other parts of the world. To know a person's name is to obtain power over him.

Tenshi means Son of Heaven, Tenno is Heavenly King. Other terms used of the Emperor are Arehito Tenno, God Walking Among Men; Kamigoichinin, Upper Exalted Foremost Being, and these lofty titles reflect the deep-seated belief of the Japanese that their nation, and especially their royal family, is heaven-descended. They derive from the gods, the sun goddess Amaterasu having particularly concerned herself with the task of creation. All other peoples descend from inferior sources. The Emperor himself is derived from the rape performed by Susanoó, the god of lust, on his sister, Amaterasu. The first emperor, Jimmu, who ascended the throne in 660 BC, was fifth in descent from this incestuous union.

Other titles of the Emperor are Dairi (Court), Gosho (Palace), Chotei (Hall of Audience); Kinri (The Forbidden Interior); Renka (The Royal Palanquin); Heika (Steps to the Throne); Aramikami (Incarnate God); Akitsukame (Manifest Destiny), this last by a strange coincidence being the term sometimes applied by Americans to the spirit, or driving force, of their own history.

One of the older western writers on Japan (J. H. Gubbins, *The Making of Modern Japan*, 1922), remarked : 'That the impersonality shrouding everything Japanese should show itself in the terms used to designate the sovereign is not surprising. Nor is it in any way strange that these should include such expressions as, The Palace, The Palace Interior, and the Household, for sovereigns are commonly spoken of in this way, the habit having its origin in respect. What is curious is that in the case of a sovereign venerated from the first as a god, and so closely associated with the native faith, the terms by which he is known to his subjects should, with

127

one exception, be borrowed from China, and that this one exception, the name Mikado, which means Honourable Gate, should be
the term least used.' Even more strange is the fact that this divinity
on earth has never been allowed to exercise much power, hardly
any in fact. Many of the emperors have lived in dire poverty, with
barely the means to keep a small household. From the earliest times
of genuine historical record in Japan, that is from the seventh
century AD, there are no instances of emperors leading their troops
into battle, making laws or even presiding at great social meetings,
such as we associate with the existence of a court. Perhaps the
monarchy very early in its history came under the control of its
great barons, but, whatever the explanation, the fact remains that
the country has been ruled from time immemorial until at least the
nineteenth century by powerful nobles or groups in whose hands
the emperor has been a puppet. The real power in Japan from early
times was exercised by the general who commanded the imperial
armies. Despite all the power which legends ascribe to their pantheon, the Japanese had to fight hard for their country against the
hairy Ainu, the aboriginal inhabitants. The title of the successful
general was Sei-i-Tai-Shogun (Barbarian-quelling General). This
was contracted to Shogun, and the real control of the state was in
the hands of the holder of the Shogunate. There were two courts,
that of the Emperor and, far more resplendent and wealthy, that
of the Shogun.

Japan during the period of the European middle ages, and indeed
right up to the nineteenth century, was in a state of feudalism. The
knighthood of Japan was at least as brave, quarrelsome, blood shed-
ding and occasionally as chivalrous as its western counterparts;
while battles as savage, ladies as lovely, and dragons and giants as
dire as any in western Europe fill the annals of Japan. The daimios,
or great vassals of the throne (the word 'daimio is part Japanese,
part Chinese and means 'great name') had their armed retainers, the
famous samurai or swordsmen, members of the military caste. The
samurai were allowed to wear two swords, and if their social inferiors
misbehaved towards them they could cut them down. The military
nobility were also termed *bushi*, hence the grim code of Bushido,
under which died so many Allied prisoners of war. A discharged or
outcast *samurai* is known as a *ronin* (literally, wave man) and there
is a famous story, *The Tale of the 47 Ronins*, which describes how
some of these wandering knights avenged their dead lord.

The Shogunate was established in the twelfth century and lasted until 1867-8. It became hereditary in certain families. At the time when the Americans and other westerners were opening Japan to the outside world, the Shogun so far overshadowed the Emperor that the existence of the latter was not suspected by the white new-comers. To complicate matters, the Shogun took the title of Taikun, or Tycoon (Great Lord), hence Japan's legacy of this term to the world of big business.

Just as the Mayors of the Palace kept the Merovingian kings in a puppet condition, so did the Shogun treat the Emperor but for a far longer period and with a much stranger sequel. None of the Shoguns made himself emperor, and at the end of the 800 years' rule they brought their tenure of office to an end. The Emperor Komei had secured the right from the Shogun to deal with foreign affairs and, when he died in 1867, he was succeeded by his son, Mutsuhito, then only fifteen. In one modern work on Japan, he is thus described : 'Born in 1852 . . . the Mikado Mutsuhito, who died on July 30, 1912, lived to see his kingdom converted into an empire, and the Japanese one of the most powerful nations on the earth. Austere, upright, calm, judicious, far-sighted and benevolent, Mut-suhito was what Plato had sighed for and Voltaire vainly sought— a philosopher on the throne. During his reign, and largely owing to his influence, the most far-reaching political and social changes were introduced.' (R. P. Porter, *Japan, The Rise of a Modern Power*, 1919, p 108.) In October 1867, the Shogun gave in his resignation to the Emperor. The throne was transferred from Kyoto to Tokyo (Yedo was the old name), and most of the feudal barons offered to surrender their estates to the Emperor, and to transfer the allegiance of their vassals. Under a series of edicts, 1871-1875, feudalism was abolished and a new system of titles was created on the western model. Japan already possessed an heraldic system which consisted in the *mon* or crest. The word 'crest' is here used in its correct meaning as opposed to the constant misuse in England where the crest is taken to mean a coat of arms. Anyone who has seen speci-mens of Japanese armour will remember the heraldic devices shown on helmet, shield or breastplate and which correspond to our crests. Japanese heraldry is an original, not a deriviate institution.

In 1884, the ancient nobility were required to give up their old titles and receive new western designations. The Japanese then used the European titles of baron, count, marquis, etc to describe their nobles. 'A House of Peers was to be a leading feature of the constitution now in course of preparation, and it was essential to create a new nobility before the institution of which it was to form a part came into operation. Some 500 peers in all were created, the number including 12 princes, 24 marquises, 74 counts, 321 viscounts, and 69 barons.' (J. H. Gubbins, *The Making of Modern Japan*, 1922.) In this typically western style peerage, prince replaced duke. There is no explanation available as to the extraordinary disproportion in the number of viscounts. In 1912 *The Japan Gazette—The Peerage of Japan* was published in Yokohama, a work clearly based on Burke or Debrett, or the *Almanach de Gotha*. Each article on a noble family is headed by the *mon*, or heraldic device of the house.

As Japanese expansion began, the first territory to be taken over was the Ryu Kyu Islands, south of Kyushu. 'The king of Ryu Kyu had for centuries led a semi-independent existence paying tribute either to China or Japan. In 1875 the Japanese Government boldly declared his kingdom a prefecture. The king himself, who was treated quite well, was created a marquis in the Japanese nobility.' (Ian Morrison, *This War against Japan*, 1943, p 24.) Along with the adoption of the European titular system, the Japanese decided to introduce a number of orders of chivalry. Hence among the others the great order of the Chrysanthemum.

Continuing with the Asian monarchies, two of our monarchical states exist on the borders of India, together with a dependent state also a monarchy. These are Bhutan and Nepal, and the dependent state of Sikkim. The rulers of these three bear the title of Maharaja (or great king), which we shall consider again in connection with the former ruling princes of India. The style of the ruler of Bhutan is HH the Maharaja. Formerly this was a dual rulership, as in Tibet, that of the Dharma Raja, who succeeded by a process of reincarnation (again as in Tibet, in the case of the Dalai Lama), and of the Deb Raja. The former was the spiritual head of Bhutan, the latter responsible for temporal affairs. In reality, the governors of east and west Bhutan, known as the Pelops, were in control. In 1904 the Dharma Raja died, and in 1907 the Tongsa Pelop was elected as the first hereditary Maharaja of Bhutan. Very often the rulers of these eastern states, which were within the British sphere of influence, were granted knighthoods in the now obsolescent orders of the Indian Empire.

130

In Nepal there is an hereditary monarchy, but for over 100 years there was also a premiership hereditary in the Rana family. The rules of succession to this office were set out as though in a royal dynasty. The titular sovereign was the Maharaja Dhiraj. The prime minister was styled His Highness the Maharaja. The last of the Rana premiers resigned in 1952, when a more democratic type of constitution came into being.

With Sikkim (included here for geographical convenience), the Indian Government has by a treaty of 1950 continued the relationship which formerly existed between that country and the British. Sikkim is thus a protectorate of India and does not rank as a sovereign independent state, though it still possesses an hereditary monarchy. All three of these northern states are Buddhist in religion, as is also Thailand, or Siam. The latter was formerly the preserve of an absolute monarchy, but since 1932 a constitutional government has prevailed. The style of the sovereign is HM, and for members of the royal house HRH. The reigning family dates from 1782, when a successful general was proclaimed king.

Indochina has disappeared as a name on the map, and in place of it we have Viet Minh, Viet Nam, Laos and Cambodia. Viet Minh is the northern portion of Cochin China, Tongking and Annam; Viet Nam the southern part. Annam formerly had an emperor, Bo Dai, but a referendum in 1952 replaced him by a republic.

Cambodia was formerly part of the French Empire, but since January 1955 has been financially, economically and politically independent of France. The monarchy of Cambodia is reputedly (by tradition) very old, going back to the Khmer monarchs who built the enormous temples later overrun by the jungle until rediscovered by French archaeologists. The monarchy is now constitutional. So, too, is the kingdom of Laos which, like Cambodia, was under French tutelage but has now regained its independence.

In these Asiatic states we have been dealing with Buddhism, but reaching Afghanistan, another neighbour of India, we find a militant Moslem country. The history of Afghanistan is exceedingly stormy, the Afghans being a brave, warlike and cruel people, very greatly attached to their Islamic faith. In recent decades their monarchy has exhibited all the usual ingredients of oriental history. King Amanullah, after a preliminary war with Britain (the third in our history), came on a visit to Europe in 1927. In 1929 he was driven

131

from his throne into exile, lucky to have escaped with his life. The influence of the mullahs (the term used rightly to describe the Moslem theologians and jurists but quite wrongly as 'priests'), was all against him. That his queen had appeared in public and unveiled could not have helped him. The local chiefs feared that they would lose their independence. Religious and political influences combined to provoke a rebellion against Amanullah. In his place a robber, taking the title Habibullah II, seized the throne, only to be captured and executed, whereupon Nadir Shah became King or Amir (also Ameer=commander). The latter was assassinated in 1933, and his son succeeded. Majesty is a precarious possession in this mountain land.

Iran, or Persia, is a monarchy which has lasted for 2,500 years, although the present reigning royal family dates only from 1925. A Persian officer in the Persian Cossack brigade, which he entered in 1900, Reza Shah Pahlevi organized a *coup d'etat* in order to bring to an end the degenerate Qajar dynasty. On 31 October 1925, he became Regent of the Persian Empire and head of the provisional government. The national assembly elected him as hereditary sovereign on 12 December 1925 and he was crowned on 25 April 1926. He thus became Shah-in-Shah, literally ruler of rulers, the familiar King of Kings. He could neither read nor write but proved a very able monarch until he was forced to abdicate when Britain and Russia occupied his country during the second world war. His son took his place, and his style is that of His Imperial Majesty Mohammed Reza Shah Pahlevi, Shah-in-Shah of Persia (the King of Kings, the Light of the Aryans). The coronation of the Shah did not take place until 27 October 1967, although he had then been well over twenty years on the throne. Delay was said to be due to the Shah having deferred his coronation until he had a son and heir. The Shah crowned himself and then crowned his Queen and Empress.

Jordan, Saudi Arabia and the Yemen are Moslem monarchies. Jordan is known in full as the Hashemite kingdom of Jordan and the ancestors of the royal house were hereditary Emirs of Mecca from 1201. The ruler of Transjordan was at first (after the 1914-18 war) described as Emir of that country, but in 1946 Transjordan was recognized as a sovereign state and the Emir became King.

Saudia Arabia includes the holy cities of Islam—Mecca and Medina. Ibn Saud, who died in 1953, was King of Saudi Arabia

132

from 1932. He used the titles of Imam and Protector of the Faith owing to his custody of the sacred places.

To the west of Saudia Arabia lies one of the least known and most inaccessible of all countries, the Yemen, which is ruled by a 'priest' king who is at the same time the spiritual and temporal head of his subjects. His style is His Highness the Imam. Although there are no priests in Islam, the peculiar position of the Yemenite House renders the term less unrealistic than usual. Probably in Islamic theory the regime is a theocracy, with the hereditary Imam as God's representative. For some centuries the Yemen, one of the few fairly fruitful areas of Arabia, was subject to the Turkish Sultan, but after the 1914-18 war the country became independent. The ruling family, that of the Zaids, is far older than either the country's independence or its connection with the Turkish Empire. It goes back to the dissensions in the Islamic world in the times of the first Caliphs. The Zaids are chosen from among the Sayyids, or descendants of Aly, the husband of the Prophet's daughter Fatima. At present the country is heavily involved in civil war which may remove the monarchy.

Before leaving Asia one very modern figure should be noted. After the British withdrawal, the Federation of Malaya became an independent state on 31 August 1957. Under the new constitution, the rulers of the eleven Malay states elect for a term of five years one of their number who is known as the Head of State—The Yang di Pertuan Agong. He is a raja of one of the Malay states, and though obviously not an hereditary sovereign, is a sovereign of sorts.

In dealing with the three African monarchies—Morocco, Libya and Ethiopia—there are, in the first instance, two which are due to the re-emergence of Islamic powers after the 1939-45 war. Ethiopia, on the contrary, has a fair claim to be the oldest monarchy in the world.

Morocco is now a kingdom under HM Mohammed V Sidi Mohammed ben Youssef. The present royal line, that of the Shereefinans, gained the throne about the year 1660. They were known as Alaouites, or Filalis, and were both Sultans and Shereefs, ie, descendants of the Prophet Mohammed. Morocco was described as the Shereefian Empire. The greatest sovereign of the dynasty was Moulay Ismail, who reigned from 1672 to 1727. He was abominably cruel, and of his hundreds of sons, any who showed signs of ability

133

were executed. A story is told of Moulay's way of gratifying the wishes of one of his courtiers, who had complained of the stench coming from below the palace. The Sultan or Emperor (barbarian, as Gibbon calls him) informed the man that he should be raised above all such matters. He was, being impaled while still alive at the highest point of the palace.

Into this land of beauty and savagery, culture and bestiality, came the civilizing power of France, and from 1912 to 1956 Morocco was a French protectorate. The French intervened in 1830 in Algeria and from Algiers they were forced to take over the whole of the huge area from the Atlantic shore of Morocco to the borders of Libya. The north of Morocco was administered as a Spanish province, with Tangier having a special international status. The present King of Morocco became Sultan in 1927, was exiled by the French in 1953, but recalled by them and reinstated in 1955. In 1956 Morocco secured its independence from France and became a kingdom.

Libya was a province of the old Turkish Empire which was conquered by the Italians in 1911. The tribesmen, the Senussi, were never reconciled to Italian rule, and after the end of the second world war their leader, the Grand Senussi, became King of Libya as Idris I. The founder of the family was Sayed Mohammed Ali ibn-es-Senussi, who was said to be descended from an old Spanish aristocratic family. He had been born near Tlemcen, in Algeria, in 1787, and had great success among the tribesmen of the North African desert. He became the Grand Senussi. He died in 1860, and was succeeded by his son, and later by his grandson, now King Idris I. The latter was born in 1889 in Cyrenaica, and was at first accepted by the Italians as Emir of Cyrenaica. In 1923 they turned against him and he was exiled. In 1943, when the German and Italian forces were finally driven from Libya, the Emir returned and was confirmed in the Emirate by the British. By the Peace Treaty signed in 1947, the Italians renounced all claims to their former possessions in Africa. The future of these territories was to be settled by the four Great Powers—USA, Britain, France and USSR—but agreement proved impossible and the case was submitted to the General Assembly of the United Nations. The British Government recognized the Emir, Mohammed Sayed Idris el-Senussi, as Emir of Cyrenaica; he proclaimed the independence of Libya and eventually the United Nations resolved that Libya should become an independent sovereign state by 1 January 1952. The National Assembly of Libya proclaimed the Emir as King of Libya.

The title of the sovereign of Ethiopia is His Imperial Majesty Haile Selassie I (Tafari Makonnen) Emperor, Negusa Nagasti (King of the Kings) of Ethiopia. This title of King of Kings, as with that of the Shah of Persia, does not imply a Nebuchadnezzar-like pride of dominion but expresses a fact, the ruler's supremacy over his vassal kings. The Rases were the great feudal barons of Ethiopia.

The life of the Emperor has been extremely chequered. Proclaimed King in 1928 and Emperor in 1930, he was in 1936 driven from his country by the Italians and his title of Emperor of Ethiopia was given to the King of Italy by Mussolini. In 1940, the real emperor had the satisfaction of seeing the British forces begin the task of reducing the Italians, who were overcome by 1941. The Emperor was then restored to his throne.

The styles of the Ethiopian royal family are Prince and Princess, His or Her Imperial Highness. The heir is the Crown Prince. The title of Duke is used, as with the late Duke of Harar, a younger son of the emperor, who died in 1957.

The origin of this royal family is most romantic. The Ethiopians believe that their emperor is the descendant of King Solomon and the Queen of Sheba, the Queen of the South as she is called in the New Testament. Three thousand years of royalty! No other pedigree in the whole world can equal this. Can the claim be made good? Amazingly enough, the claim was formulated in writing as far back as the early centuries of the present era, before any of the European monarchies had been founded out of the wreckage of the dissolving Roman Empire. The *Kebra Nagast*, or *Glory of Kings*, is the very early Ethiopian work which gives the story of Solomon and Sheba. The authors make no claim; what they state has for them the equivalance of gospel truth. The *Glory of Kings* dates from about the fourth century AD but a scholar of the eminence of Sir Wallis Budge, who translated the whole book, considered that before the appearance of the volume which he translated there had existed other versions which went back to an even more ancient date, while the tradition serving as base for all the editions was of a very remote age in Ethiopia. Here is the story: Queen Makeda of Ethiopia is renowned as a trader in the lands around the Red Sea. The leader of her caravans, named Tamrin, trades with the kingdom of Israel. Solomon is at this time building the Temple at Jerusalem and the

135

fame of his magnificent greatness is spread far and wide, so that Tamrin regales his mistress with tales of Solomon's wonders. Desirous of seeing this marvellous ruler, Makeda journeys to Jerusalem and is much impressed by Solomon's wisdom and beauty of appearance. So far the story is that of the Old Testament narrative, but now comes the peculiarly Ethiopian portion. Solomon and Makeda fall in love, but for some unspecified reason she resists his desire to enjoy her person. At last by a trick but without force, Solomon has his way. In due course Makeda returns to her own country, having promised that a son from the marriage (apparently the consummation was followed by a formal union) shall be sent to Solomon after the boy has reached manhood. A son named Menelik is born and visits Solomon, who receives him with great consideration. When Menelik is about to return to Ethiopia he asks his father for a fringe of the covering of the Ark. Solomon refuses but by a skilful plan Menelik secures possession of the real Ark and substitutes a counterfeit. He then returns home and reigns as Menelik, or David II. The book concludes with this fervent paragraph:

'Thus hath God made for the King of Ethiopia more glory and grace and majesty than for all the other kings of the earth because of the greatness of Zion, the Tabernacle of the Law of God, the heavenly Zion. And may God make us to perform His spiritual good pleasure and deliver us from His wrath and make us to share His kingdom. Amen.'

The line of kings from Solomon and Makeda is said to have continued unbroken until the tenth century AD, when it was interrupted by the usurpation of the Zague kings from 914 to 1268, after which the Solomonic line was restored.

Such is this extraordinary story. For many ages the Ethiopians believed that the sacred Ark of Israel with the Tablets of the Testimony given by God to Moses was kept at Aksum. At least this account would explain the fate of the Ark on which the Old Testament is silent, although it gives many details as to the history of the far less important vessels of the Temple. The whole history of Ethiopia is of fascinating interest, and those who would know more about this most ancient monarchy which has survived to the present day should read the translation of the late Sir Wallis Budge, *The Queen of Sheba and her only son, Menelik*, (1922).

Although the ruling power which held sway in Tibet before the Chinese conquest cannot claim even a third of the age of the

Ethiopian royal house, it has a property unknown elsewhere in the world, unless we are prepared to regard the Emperor of Japan as a divine being and the central figure in the national religion of Shintoism. For that is what the *de jure* sovereign of Tibet is in fact —the heart and centre of a religion, Lamaism or Tibetan Buddhism. A lama is a Tibetan or Mongolian Buddhist priest and the Dalai, or Great Lama is the traditional ruler of Tibet, a combination of king and priest. The Panchen Lama is the other great spiritual force in Tibet and is head of the great monastery, the Mount of Blessing. He was or is regarded as the incarnation of the celestial Buddha, Boundless Light. Chen-re-Zi, the tutelary deity of Tibet, whose incarnation the Dalai Lama is held to be, was the spiritual son of the Celestial Buddha. There are also other lamas 'in whom' remarks an acute western observer 'the emanation from some deity or bygone saint is present in an occult manner. But the high spiritual essence and the overwhelming secular power which the Dalai Lama has inherited render him supreme.' (Sir Charles Bell, *Portrait of the Dalai Lama*, 1946.) There is also a Tashi Lama in Mongolia. The name of the present incarnation of the Dalai Lama is : The Holy One, The Gentle Glory, Powerful in Speech, Pure in Mind, of Divine Wisdom, Holding the Faith, Ocean Wide.

The position of the Dalai Lama invites comparison with that of the Pope. An obvious parallel is found between the assistance given to the Popes in the eighth and ninth centuries by the French rulers and the help rendered to the temporal authority of the priest kings by the Mongolian chiefs.

Besides the sovereigns referred to above, there are several oriental potentates who should be mentioned, the rulers of the Sultanates and Sheikhdoms of East Africa and the Persian Gulf. The Sultan of Muscat and Oman belongs to the dynasty of Al Abu Said, which was established in 1741. From this family has also come the Sultanate of Zanzibar, now superseded by the republic of Tanzania, formed between Tanganyika, Zanzibar and Pemba.

There are on the Persian Gulf in eastern Arabia seven sheikhdoms. The word 'sheikh' is an Arabic term meaning an elder or chief. In modern English it has acquired an association of romance which has no basis in reality and is characteristic of the strange tendency of the British people over the last 100 years to idealize the Arabs, a trait previously confined to a few oriental travellers. The sheikhdoms are known as the Trucial States because, under British influence, the various sheikhs have sworn a perpetual truce, their motives not being unconnected with the discovery of oil in the region. These sheikhdoms are Abu Dhabi; Dubai; Sharja and Kalba; Ras al-Khaimah; Ajman; Umm Al Quwain, and Fujaira. Larger sheikhdoms further along the Gulf towards Persia are those of Qatar, Bahrain and Kuwait. The style of these sheikhs is His Highness.

NOTE: Sovereignty. It is interesting to recall that claims to very extensive ownership and sovereignty over the seas and oceans surrounding, or adjacent to a country were formerly made. From a fairly distant period the English kings were wont to claim lordship of the narrow seas around the shores of England, particularly the English Channel. In this connection, it is significant that the English are, I believe, the only people to call this sea by their own name. Numerous quarrels with other nations have arisen from the English claim. When England's seapower has been great, the claim has been acknowledged, albeit grudgingly. The affray in the time of Edward III between that king's fleet and a Spanish fleet in the Channel was caused by what the English monarch regarded as the insolent behaviour of the Iberians. In the period of the Anglo-Dutch wars of the seventeenth century, the supremacy in the narrow seas eventually remained with England, after a struggle which swayed backwards and forwards, with England receiving some severe blows.

Under the early Stuarts, some of the claims to sea ownership were fantastic. The doctrine of the *Mare Clausum* expounded by John Selden would have given the sovereignty of most of the Atlantic Ocean and the North Sea to Britain. A more realistic and sensible view was enunciated by the celebrated Hugo Grotius. In time, this came to be adopted, and the sea, that most uncontrollable of all elements, remained free. In the eighteenth century, the territorial waters of a country were limited to three miles from the shore, the distance a cannon ball could reach. In our time, several nations have exceeded this limit and the dispute of some years back between Iceland and Britain over the former's extension of its territorial waters to twelve miles from shore is only one illustration of the modern approach. Some South American states claim to control the waters to some 200 miles from their shores, in a manner distantly reminiscent of Selden's doctrines.

The term 'high seas' is much used and is held in English law to include the whole of the sea below low-water mark and outside the body of a country. Thus the realm of England extends only to the low-water mark, and everything beyond this constitutes the high seas. The definition of territorial waters is given in the Territorial Waters Jurisdiction Act, 1878, which is described as 'An Act to regulate the law relating to the Trial of Offences committed on the Sea within a certain distance of the coasts of Her Majesty's Dominions.' In Section 7, which deals with interpretation of terms, the term, 'territorial waters' of the Queen's dominions is thus defined. It means in reference to the sea, 'such part of the sea adjacent to the coast of the United Kingdom or the coast of some other part of Her Majesty's dominions, as is deemed by international law to be within the territorial sovereignty of Her Majesty; and for the purpose of any offence declared by this Act to be within the jurisdiction of the Admiral any part of the open sea within one marine league of the coast measured from low-water mark shall be deemed to be open sea within the territorial waters of Her Majesty's dominions'.

The interest of nations in the seas has turned on freedom of movement across them and, of course, on freedom to fish in them. In this latter respect, the humble herring is supposed to have been a prime mover in the downfall of Charles I. That king, actuated as always by the best motives, was anxious to protect his fishermen as they went about their lawful occasions. The herring shoals tended to move from their original spawning grounds, and British fishermen, in following them, were liable to come into collision with fishing fleets of other nations. Charles therefore built a powerful fleet. The price of admiralty in this instance entailed taxation which Charles' subjects felt to be excessive and unwarranted. Hence the great Civil War and the subsequent melancholy scene outside Charles' own palace of Whitehall on 30 January 1649. In our dispute with Iceland the Royal Navy sailed to support our fishing fleet, but the mid-twentieth century outcome was a conference of maritime nations followed by Britain's withdrawal from her claim to uphold the three-mile limit.

12. Indian Titles

Although the magnificence of the ruling princes of India is now a matter of past glory, there are still Indian princes who retain at least the styles, though no longer the power of their predecessors. To obtain information about their styles is far from easy. A huge volume of literature still remains dusty and now almost unread in the archives of various institutions. The British who resided in the old Empire were not incurious about it, and their efforts to learn about the history and antiquities of India were not without success. They were even approved by Indians. A Rajput prince presented me with that huge compendium, *The Annals and Antiquities of Rajasthan*, written by Colonel James Tod who, in 1812, was appointed political agent in Rajputana. An amusing sketch exists showing the colonel sitting with his Jain Pundit, and obviously absorbing information; this book is now a classic and a work in which it is possible to lose oneself, simply reading for the interest. Rajputana was, however, only a small section of princely India. To quote from *The Princes of India* by Sir William Barton, KCIE, CSI, with an introduction by Viscount Halifax, former Viceroy (1934, p xiii) : 'One-third of the surface of India and more than a fourth of its population are outside British jurisdiction . . . The Indian States number 562, of which 327 are relatively of very little consequence, and only exist independently as the result of an historical accident.'

Indian titles fall into three sections : Hindu, Moslem, and super-imposed on these, western and English styles, the result of the British domination of India. In the beginning of the eleventh century Mahmud the Image Breaker, a fierce and capable Moslem leader, succeeded in conquering northern India. This was the first Moslem invasion and although the Moslems did not conquer the whole of India, and their power declined before a resurgence of Hinduism, they nonetheless made a deep impact upon Indian life. Then, in

140

the autumn of 1398, the Mongol conqueror, Timur the Lame, invaded India and made Delhi the scene of some of his most horrible massacres. Just over 100 years later a Turk named Baur (meaning 'The Lion'), who claimed descent paternally from Timur and maternally from Jenghiz Khan, began the establishment of the Mogul Empire in India. (Mogul is a Persian form of Mongol.) There were several great princes in this line, Akbar being perhaps the most outstanding. He practised toleration in religious matters and seems to have adopted a syncretic policy in religion, choosing those portions of each faith which appealed to him. By 1690 the Mogul emperor, Aurungzeb, had succeeded in overrunning the whole of southern India, and the empire could be said to extend from the Himalayas to Cape Comorin. The dominion was short-lived and in the decay and decline of the Mogul power in the eighteenth century the majority of the native princedoms arose.

Another consequence of the anarchic state of India 250 years ago was that it gave opportunity to Europeans to intervene in the affairs of the country. Beginning as traders, both French and English gradually became involved in Indian politics, and as France and England were often at war it was natural for their quarrels to find an outlet in India. In due time the paramount power was that of England, wielded through the Honourable East India Company. The story of the former ruling princes of India is that of sovereigns who found themselves under the necessity of seeking the protection of an overlord. So it was that a form of feudalism developed, with the British as the suzerain and responsible for the foreign affairs of the Indian states. The Mogul emperor continued as a figurehead—the King of Delhi—until after the Indian Mutiny when, in 1858, Bahadur Shah, the last of the Moguls, was tried for complicity with the mutineers and banished to Rangoon. This was the end of the line of Great Moguls, as the emperors were called, literally, the Great Mongolian. How curious a fate that a now out-of-the-way country should have produced so many terrible conquerors to ravage Europe and Asia almost at will. Incidentally, the famous Peacock Throne now used by the Shah of Persia was originally that of the Great Mogul and was carried off to Persia by Nadir Shah in 1739.

When one studies works on India, even when they are written by highly experienced administrators, the impression gained concerning titles is that they were haphazardly awarded. Some rulers were given the style of Highness, some of His Excellency, others

141

were awarded no prefix at all. Knighthoods in a variey of British orders appear in ill-regulated profusion, and the possible explanation is perhaps that of Kipling, that the undecorated prince had failed to catch his Viceroy's eye. The relationship between the Crown and the princes was strongly reminiscent of medieval feudalism in Europe. 'The official view was that the previous sanction of the Viceroy was necessary to the succession. The princes, on their part, while admitting that the recognition of the British Government was necessary, demur to the principle of prior sanction.' (Sir William Barton, *op cit*, p 264.) 'The Crown exercises the right, through the Viceroy, to recognise successions, to assume the guardianship of minors, to confer or withdraw titles, decorations and salutes, to sanction the acceptance of foreign orders and to grant passports. In 1860 a table of salutes was published.'

The history of the rules governing the grant of titles to the princes is somewhat complicated. Before 1889, the Government of India appears to have employed no particular system or generally accepted rules in the titles it bestowed on ruling princes. In 1889, after lengthy considerations, the Governor General in Council decided to restrict the title of High Highness to rulers who were entitled to a salute of not less than ten guns, whether permanent or personal, and also to certain Indian noblemen and ladies (about twenty in number) named in a special list. It was further intimated to all authorities concerned that, as a matter of courtesy, the lawful and recognized widows and wives of all persons entitled to style themselves Highness should likewise be addressed by that title at the same time; the title of His Excellency, which had previously been applied to certain rulers, virtually lapsed from official usage.

The rules promulgated in 1889 were apparently applied to all the Indian princes and ruling chiefs, with one exception, until revised in 1925. During the period 1889-1925 the number of Indian noblemen and ladies for whom the rules of 1889 provided the title of Highness as a personal distinction sharply declined for various reasons. In 1925 the Indian Government, with the approval of the Secretary of State for India, decided that in future the titles of His Highness and Her Highness should be confined to ruling princes enjoying salutes of eleven guns and over, to their lawful wives and widows, and to the then Yuvaraj of Mysore. The new rules also declared that the claims of the successors of the Indian notables who were not ruling princes but were accorded the title of Highness as a personal distinction would be considered on their merits. Ordinarily the title would only be renewed for very exceptional reasons.

The 1925 rules remained officially in force until 1947; it is interesting to observe that with effect from 13 November 1936, the Heir Apparent to HEH the Nizam of Hyderabad was granted the title of His Highness the Prince of Berar by the King Emperor. The province of Berar was the richest part of the Nizam's dominions and when, in the earlier part of the nineteenth century, the Nizam's finances had become nearly bankrupt, it was very hard to raise sufficient money to maintain the troops deemed necessary by the British Government for the preservation of order. 'In the end, the arrears were so heavy that the Indian Government insisted on an assignment of territory as security for payment. The Berars . . . was taken over in 1853 for the purpose. Even with this the arrears amounted to eleven millions of rupees after the Mutiny. They were cancelled in recognition of the Nizam's services, and it was agreed that the surplus of the Berars revenue, after meeting the cost of the Contingent, should be paid over to the Hyderabad Government.' (Barton, *op cit*, p 194.) In 1902 the Viceroy (Lord Curzon) persuaded the Nizam to lease the Berars in perpetuity in return for a quit rent of twenty lakhs of rupees. Perhaps the conferment of the title from this lost province was an additional *douceur*. By 1947, the date of the hand-over of authority by Britain, it had become fairly common social practice for ruling princes with salutes of nine guns to be addressed as His Highness. According to a Government of India Political Department Notification of 6 August 1947, the use of the styles of His Highness and Her Highness was extended to all rulers of Indian states with salutes of nine guns and to their lawful wives and widows.

Before giving a brief resumé of the history of the Indian states, the principal native titles can be dealt with. Raja(h), the most familiar to English ears, comes from the Hindustani *raj*, to reign (hence the British Raj), and so the meaning of a 'king'. Ranee or Rani, Queen, is the female counterpart of Raja, and Rajput means 'son of a king'. Maharaja(h) means 'great king'. These are Hindu titles. Nawab is a Moslem title denoting a native governor or nobleman in India, being the Hindustani, *nawwab*. In the English language it has also commonly been rendered as nabob, meaning a wealthy, retired Anglo-Indian, more particularly of the eighteen century. A Moslem title is the well-known Nizam, which comes from a word of Arabic origin meaning 'order' or 'arrangement'. The Peshwa (Persian, chief) was used of the hereditary sovereign of the Mahratta state. The very well-known Sahib was a term applied by Indians to Europeans, and came from Arabic into Hindustani, meaning 'friend'. It was appended to the surname, as Jones Sahib. The term Sahib-log denoted Europeans in general. Bahadur was another title used in connection with the names of officers, and having the sense of 'brave'.

The ruling houses of India and Pakistan have come into existence at widely separated times, and almost all owe their origin to success of arms. Hardly any of the states, including the non-salute states of the ruling chiefs, were grants or creations. The salute states of the ruling princes had their own nobility and vassalage, and these nobles were sometimes known as Thakurs. When at the time of British rule in India an Indian state sought British protection, a British guarantee was sometimes interposed between, eg, the Marathas, the tributary Rajput states and the feudal barons. States thus treated were termed mediatised, an interesting similarity with the procedure which was being adopted about the same time in Europe in what had been the Holy Roman Empire. Under these arrangements, tribute and services were fixed and, provided these were duly rendered, the feudatories were protected against their feudal overlords and their authority was maintained in their own territories.

Rajput Princes. The origin of some of the princely houses is said to be lost in antiquity, the Rajput dynasties, which established themselves in Rajasthan and Saurashtra in the tenth and eleventh centuries, trace their descent from the Kshatriya heroes of the Hindu Epics, the *Ramayana* and the *Mahabharata*. They connect their genealogies with the Puranic genealogies of the ancient Kings and *Rishis* but Colonel James Tod, in his famous *Annals and Antiquities of Rajasthan,* suggests that the Rajputs are descended from the White Huns who invaded India in several waves, the largest taking place in AD 999 under Toramana and his son, Mihiragula. The genealogies from this time on are certainly better authenticated. Traditionally, there are thirty-six royal races of the Rajputs with a recognised head of each race or clan. The clans are strictly exogamous. The Rajputs conquered and ruled over an area of some 150,000 square miles.

The traditional leader of the Rajputs is His Highness the Maharana of Udaipur (Rana is the name of a Rajput chief), who claims descent from Rama (cf the semi-divine descendents of the ancient kings in western Europe). His Highness' forebear, the gallant Rana Pratep, led the Rajput resistance against Mogul encroachments under the Emperor Akbar; his personal trials and heroism have become a saga of Rajput chivalry. Since that time the Maharanas have been saluted with the distinctive style significant of Hindu premiership : Hindu'a Suraj, 'Sun of the Hindus'.

Deccan Princes. His Exalted Highness the Nizam of Hyderabad enjoys the highest precedence among the princes. He was seventh in descent from the founder of the state, Asif Jah, who was the last Mogul Viceroy of the Deccan. His Exalted Highness' dominions comprised an area of 82,000 square miles. The titles of His Exalted Highness and of 'Faithful Ally of the British Government' were conferred on the Nizam in recognition of his great services to Britain from 1914 to 1919, not only in the world war but also in keeping Indian Moslems calm during the subsequent Afghan war.

Two other important states in the Deccan were Mysore, with an area of 30,000 square miles and Travancore, with an area of 8,000 square miles. In Travancore the dynastic succession passes through the female line.

Mahratta Princes. The other large block of states in India was that of the Mahrattas, the remnants of the Mahratta Confederacy which had almost the whole of India in its grip during the interregnum between the end of the Mogul Raj and the beginning of the British. Under the indomitable Shivaji, whose capital was at Poona, the Mahrattas began their wars against the Emperor Aurungzeb, and these did not end until the final overthrow and collapse of the Mogul Empire. The Confederacy was itself broken up by internal dissensions and, in the last phase, by the advent of British arms. The widely scattered area that remained under the Mahrattas was about 47,000 square miles.

The premier Mahratta princes are Their Highnesses the Maharaja Gaekwar of Baroda, who takes precedence immediately after the Nizam, the Maharaja Scindia of Gwalior, and the Maharaja Holkar of Indore. The ruler who receives the formal deference of all the Mahrattas, as successor to the House of Shivaji, is His Highness the Maharaja Chhatrapati of Kolahpur. Many years ago Queen Victoria conferred on the Gaekwar the title of 'Favourite Son of the Empire'.

Sikh Princes. The formidable Sikh power of the Punjab was

broken after a long series of wars and the area remaining under princely rule was 10,000 square miles. The foremost Sikh prince is His Highness the Maharaja of Patiala.

The Sikhs were originally the followers, or disciples, of a man named Kabir in about 1500; the name Sikh meaning 'follower'. Kabir and those gurus (teachers) who succeeded him, at first endeavoured to reconcile Hinduism and Islam and any other faith of which they had knowledge. At first, too, they were pacifists, and it was only the persecution of Aurungzeb which turned them into the military race they became and as which they are so well known throughout the world. Under the last Guru (1675-1708), they were organised into a warlike sect and each Sikh added the word Singh (still used by all to this day) to his name, to signify 'lion', that is, bravery. From this time, too, date the practices, such as uncut hair, which still distinguish the Sikhs.

Kashmir. The state of Jammu and Kashmir, with its 82,000 square miles, is a disputed territory between India and Pakistan. The Kashmir dynasty are Dogra Rajputs. Gulab Singh, Raja of Jammu, was a general in the Sikh armies and later a prime minister of Maharaja Ranjit Singh, King of the Punjab. He conquered Kashmir and his sovereignty over it was recognised by the British under the Treaty of Amritsar in 1846. The state is at present divided along a cease-fire line between India and Pakistan.

Moslem States. These may fairly be described as succession states to the Mogul Empire, and there are about a dozen of them. Bhopal, the most important Moslem state next to Hyderabad, was founded by an Afghan adventurer, Dost Mohammed, about 300 years ago. The Nizam of Hyderabad greatly assisted his son, Yur Mohammed, in gaining his father's throne. He conferred on the new prince the decoration of the Mahi Maratib, the dignity of the Fish, a high honour of the Mogul Empire which still forms the main item in the coat of arms of Bhopal.

The present position of the ruling princes of India and Pakistan is governed by the fact that, in the past, they had treaty relations with the British Crown and were recognised as sovereigns of their states. On the lapse of the British paramountcy in 1947, the rulers executed Instruments of Accession to one of the two new Dominions for purposes of foreign relations, defence and communications. In the period 1948-50 most of the states acceding to India formed themselves into unions of states, or joined with neighbouring provinces for administrative purposes. The Rajpramukh (Governor) of a union of states is elected by the covenanting rulers from among themselves.

Under the covenants and agreements by which the Indian rulers resigned their sovereignties over their several territories they and their families continue to enjoy, under guarantee from the Government of India, the personal privileges, dignities and titles to which they were previously entitled. The transfer had not affected the ex-officio positions of rulers as actual or titular heads of universities, societies, orders, temples, regiments etc.

The Government of India have agreed that, subject to such essential adjustments as may be inevitable in the new set-up of India, the precedence of salute rulers *inter-se* and *vis-a-vis* officers and other persons, as it existed before 15 August 1947, will not be changed to the rulers' detriment. All customary ceremonies consistent with the dignity of the rulers are to be obsevred. The right to hold durbars (courts) is recognised, subject to the proviso that 'save in the case of Rajpramukhs' durbars, attendance will be voluntary. On ceremonial occasions, a salute of guns is fired for salute rulers. Those princes who had their own regular troops are, under the Indian States Forces scheme, furnished a guard of honour on special occasions, and a military guard at their residences, subject to the exigencies of the service. Princes enjoy certain diplomatic privileges and are provided with credentials from the President when travelling abroad. Rulers with a permanent salute of thirteen guns and over are treated as special entreé guests at Government House and are received in a separate room by the President and Governors. During the British rule, these princes enjoyed the privilege of a return visit from His Majesty the King Emperor and they continue, to the present day, to be received at the Entree Entrance of Buckingham Palace. They have the right to use Diplomatic Corps plates on their vehicles, and all rulers in India have special registration plates bearing the names of their states.

The rulers' privy purses are exempt from income tax and super-tax. Rulers with a permanent salute of nineteen guns and over may import articles for the personal use of themselves and their families free of customs and any other duties. Rulers with a permanent salute of eleven guns and over are exempt from customs and other duties on their personal luggage and belongings while returning from any place within India or abroad. Rulers' families are exempt

147

from the Arms Act and from certain processes of courts of law. They have free, and in some cases, exclusive fishing and shooting rights in their states.

Salute princes and their consorts are addressed as Your Highness; non-salute chiefs and their consorts as Maharaja(h) Sahib, Rani Sahib as the case may be; and sons and daughters of rulers as Kumar Sahib and Kumari Sahiba.

In addition to the former princes of India, there were other minor rulers who were recognized by the Government of India and on whom titles and salutes of guns were bestowed. There were seven border states on the frontier of British India and of Afghanistan. Kalat, in Baluchistan, had a Khan as its ruler; he and the Mehtar of Chitral were accorded the title of Highness and a salute of nineteen and eleven guns respectively. Swat and Phulera were two of the other states in this category.

Then there is the position of His Highness the Aga Khan, which is quite extraordinary. The chapter dealing with Moslem titles referred to the quarrels between Sunnis and Shias in Islam, and it is a variety of the Shias who are ruled by the Aga Khan. The present Aga Khan is the fourth of his line, having succeeded in July 1957. The ancestry of the Aga is traced from Fatima, the daughter of Mohammed, who married Aly, the fourth of the Caliphs. The descent is traced through the Fatimid Caliphs of Egypt and the Qajar dynasty of Persia. The present Aga Khan is the fiftieth Imam or religious leader of the Ismaili sect. The differences between the Ismailis and the remaining Shiites is that while the latter accept the line of succession through the Prophet's descendants, the Ismailis stop at the seventh generation, not at the twelfth as do the rest of the Shiites. The title of Aga Khan is secular and means Master Chief, Aga being from the Turkish and denoting a commander, or chief officer in the Ottoman Empire. The great grandfather of the present Aga, Hasan Ali Shah, was born in Persia in 1800 and was a highly-placed official, being governor of a province. He incurred the displeasure of the Shah and had to flee from Persia to India. There he was well received by the British Government and gave great assistance to British arms in Afghanistan and in Sind. He was duly recognised by the Indian Government as head of the Ismaili sect. He died in 1881 and was succeeded by his son, who survived him by only four years. In 1885 his only son, then a child eight years old, succeeded to the title and to the vast wealth of the family.

148

This great fortune is derived from the offerings of the faithful, who number some ten millions and for whom it is a religious duty to send a contribution to their chief.

The third Aga was one of the world's best-known personalities. A great lover of horse racing, he was five times the owner of a Derby winner, which probably made him better known than his considerable contributions to the political life of his times. His full title was His Highness the Aga Sultan Sir Mohammed Shah, GCSI, GCIE, GCVO, GCMG. He rendered great services to the Allied cause in the 1914 war when he rallied his followers to resist German aggression, and as Turkey, the chief Moslem power, had sided with Germany, the influence of the Aga was all the more important. In recognition of his services he was given the privilege of a salute of eleven guns. Under his will he appointed to succeed him his grandson, Karim, who is the son of Aly Khan, the late Aga's elder son. The rule of the Aga Khan corresponds to that of a Pope rather than a secular sovereign. The great interest of the Aga Khan's position is that it perpetuates the struggle for the Caliphate in the seventh and eighth centuries. In a sense, Aly has at last triumphed, for now no Caliphate exists in Islam while the Aga Khan, Aly's descendant, is respected by all Moslems. The title of the Aga's wife is the Begum Aga Khan, being the style of a Moslem princess, or lady of rank.

NOTE: In the above account of the Indian princes I have quoted the arrangements as made soon after the termination of British rule. It is perhaps not strictly necessary to state that the former rulers now possess no power in their states. They are, as a recent writer has called them, 'pensioners without power or privilege.' (See an excellent article, 'The Indian States under the British Crown', by William Seymour, in *History Today*, December 1967.) Since this chapter was finished it has been announced (*The Times*, 25 July 1968) that the Indian Government has taken a firm decision to abolish the privy purses and privileges granted to the princes on the merger of their states in the Indian Union.

13. Ecclesiástical Titles

'And there was also a strife among them, which of them should be accounted the greatest. And He said unto them, The Kings of the Gentiles exercise lordship over them; and they that exercise authority upon them are called benefactors. But ye shall not be so; but he that is greatest among you let him be as the younger; and he that is chief as he that doth serve.' (St Luke, ch 22 vs 24-26.) By contrast, we may consider the style of the most important ecclesiastic in the world : Our Most Holy Lord, His Holiness Paul VI, Bishop of Rome, Vicar of Jesus Christ, Metropolitan of the Roman Province, Primate of Italy, Patriarch of the West, and Head of the Universal Church.

Whatever objections may be raised by clergy of other Christian bodies to the Pope's titles, they are objections of theological not Gospel principle, for as we saw in the title of the Patriarch of Alexandria (page 7), in some respects his style exceeds that borne by the Bishops of Rome. Nor did the Reformation with all its changes bring the Christian clergy back to the ideal proclaimed by Christ. Reverends, Right Reverends and Most Reverends abound in the Protestant churches. Christendom is united in rejecting the precepts of its Founder, which is not surprising since in our day learned theologians abound offering explanations of Christ's words which show that He did not mean what He most plainly said.

Perhaps in the ecumenical movement now everywhere gaining momentum, and in the mania for change which accompanies it, someone may be bold enough to suggest the quiet dropping of all ecclesiastical styles beyond those of simple office. Meanwhile, the subject of ecclesiastical titles is full of interest and one wonders why Selden omitted any reference to them.

Beginning with the august personage who presides over the Catholic Church, the titles of the Pope are steeped in history. The term Pope means 'father', and up to the fifth century it was used of any bishop. In the West, it became restricted to the Bishop of Rome,

150

while in the East it was officially reserved to the Patriarchs of Alexandria, Antioch, Jerusalem and Constantinople. In popular usage it is still given to the ordinary parish priests of the Eastern, or Greek Orthodox Church. The title of Pope, though universally applied in the West to the Bishop of Rome, is not as a rule employed in formal documents. The ordinary signature of documents is *Paulus PP. VI*, ie, Paul, *Pastor pastorum*, shepherd of shepherds, VI. The signature on a Bull would be *Paulus Episcopus Ecclesiae Catholicae*, while the heading would be *Paulus Episcopus servus servorum Dei* (Servant of the servants of God). The latter title was taken by St Gregory the Great (590-604), 1,350 years ago. Other styles met in formal documents are : *Pontifex* (Pontiff), *Pontifex Maximus* (Chief Pontiff, a title derived from the emperors of pagan Rome, who were automatically priests of the pagan cult), *Summus Pontifex, Romanus Pontifex. Sanctissimus* (Most Holy). *Sanctissimus Pater* (Most Holy Father). *Sanctissimus dominus noster* (Our Most Holy Lord). *Sanctitas Sua* (His Holiness). *Beatissimus Pater* (Most Blessed Father).

These styles have grown up over the nineteen centuries of Christian history. Some have come from pagan sources, others have evolved as the ecclesiastical pyramid with the Pope at its apex has risen tier by tier. Next in dignity to the Pope come the cardinals, who have a long and interesting history. The word comes from the Latin *cardo*, a hinge on which something turns, whence our reference to the cardinal virtues, on which conduct turns or depends. By the fifth century, the term was applied to the clergy who were attached to the principal churches of Rome, which is why a cardinal today still takes his title from such and such a church in the City. During the middle ages, the term was applied to many priests in important churches, as in cathedrals, but the title gradually came to be kept for the Roman clergy who were the counsellors of the Pope, and in 1567 Pope Pius V confined it to them exclusively.

The cardinals are known collectively as the Sacred College, though this usage did not arise until the twelfth century, and it is they who elect the Pope. There have been throughout the greater part of the history of the Cardinalate three divisions : Cardinal Bishops, being the bishops of the churches in the near neighbourhood of Rome; Cardinal Priests who were in charge of the various titles (ie, parish churches in Rome); and Cardinal Deacons, of whom there were originally seven. There have been many changes in the numbers of these three divisions, but in 1586 Sixtus V fixed the number of cardinal bishops at six, of cardinal priests at fifty, and of cardinal deacons at fourteen. Pope John XXIII (1958-63) decreed that henceforward all cardinals should be bishops and on Maundy Thursday 1962 he himself consecrated all the cardinals who were not then bishops.

Previously, the highest number of cardinals was seventy-six under Pius IV (1559-66) whereas today the College numbers well over 100. The greatly extended responsibilities of the Church, which are now world-wide in the fullest sense, have required a much larger quota of the highest officials. Besides this, it has been found essential that Catholics of every race and colour should be represented in the College. Not all cardinals reside in Rome, by any means; there are cardinal archbishops and bishops holding sees throughout the world, but all must come to Rome for the election of a new Pope. Since the reign of Urban VIII the cardinals have had the title of Eminence. A cardinal is addressed in writing as His Eminence Cardinal X; in speech, as Your Eminence or My Lord Cardinal. Should he be an archbishop or bishop in his episcopal see he is styled, HE Cardinal X, Archbishop of Westminster, or HE the Cardinal Archbishop of Westminster.

Legates and apostolic delegates are sent like secular ambassadors to represent the Holy See in the different states of the world. An apostolic nuncio may be likened to an ambassador; he has diplomatic status and occupies a permanent post. A delegate is sent to a country which does not have full diplomatic relations with the Holy See. The apostolic delegate to the United Kingdom is styled the Most Reverend X, Apostolic Delegate, and is addressed, like an archbishop, as Your Grace. Since the sixteenth century nuncios (literally 'messengers' from the Latin *nuntius*) have taken the place and function of *legati a latere*.

One of the peculiar titles of the Roman Catholic Church is that of Monseigneur, or Monsignor, My Lord, abbreviated almost always to Mgr, and applied to prelates. The prelates to whom the title belongs are not, as in the Church of England usage, all bishops. The word, as with another ecclesiastical title applied to some bishops —primate,* is derived from the secular usages of pagan imperial Rome. The Emperor Valerian, in his instructions *De Prelatis*, has

* Primate was applied in the fourth and fifth centuries in the Roman Empire to both secular and ecclesiastical chiefs. In 1758 it was applied by Linnaeus to an order of mammals including apes!

152

no reference to the Church but is concerned with secular dignitaries. In the fourteenth century, even a magistrate was termed a prelate, and in the earlier middle ages the term *praelatus* ('one set over'), applied to persons of varying status who possessed ecclesiastical jurisdiction. In the modern Roman Catholic Church the prelate can be in one of four classes: (i) cardinals, archbishops or bishops; (ii) abbots and superiors of monasteries or religious communities who do not administer a diocese but have spiritual jurisdiction; (iii) Roman prelates, being members of the papal court where they discharge a function though they have no episcopal jurisdiction; (iv) honorary prelates whose duties are performed far from Rome. The title of Monsignor is borne by all members of the papal household. 'Those best known in this country are the Protonotaries Apostolic, who have the privilege of celebrating Pontifical Mass wearing a mitre, and with the extra lighted candle, several times a year; the Domestic Prelates who like the Protonotaries, wear robes very much like those of a bishop; and the Privy Chamberlains. The first two categories are styled Right Reverend and the third Very Reverend. All of them, because they belong to the papal household, take precedence over canons and are entitled to wear purple stocks.' (Catholic Diary, 1965.)

In dealing with archbishops, bishops, deans, archdeacons, canons, priests and deacons we pass from ranks exclusively Roman to those which Rome shares with the Anglican Communion and with other episcopal churches. The three orders of the historic church are: bishop, priest and deacon. There were also minor orders which are still maintained in the Roman Church; ostiarius (doorkeeper), lector (reader, an office revived in the Anglican Church in 1866), exorcist, acolyte and sub-deacon. The three major orders are easily the most important and are the principal difference between the episcopalian and non-episcopalian churches. Archbishops are styled Most Reverend and His Grace the Archbishop of X. In the case of the Anglican Archbishops of Canterbury and York, they are styled Most Reverend and Right Honourable, the latter being due to their membership of the Privy Council. As with the presence of twenty-six Anglican prelates in the House of Lords, the inclusion of the two archbishops and the Bishop of London in the Privy Council, is due to the conception of former days that the Spiritual Lords were essential to the grand assemblies of the nation. Very often in other times the Most Reverend (Right Reverend) and Right Honourable were

153

reversed, but this would be wrong now. The Archbishop of York is
Primate of England, and Canterbury Primate of all England, behind
which distinction is a long history of unseemly bickering.

By an accepted usage, a bishop who has retired is correctly referred to as Bishop Gore or Archbishop Wand, but it is wrong so
to style him when he occupies his see. Most bishops, at least in the
Anglican Church, are termed Doctor, even though few now hold an
honorary doctorate. The term Lord Bishop applies strictly to the
forty-three diocesan bishops of England in the Established Church.
It is quite incorrect for any others, though all bishops—Suffragan,
Missionary, and Roman Catholic—are rightly called Right Reverend.
The same applies to Anglican bishops in the (disestablished) churches
of Ireland, and Wales, and in the Episcopal Church of Scotland.
The (Protestant) Archbishop of Armagh is Primate of All Ireland,
the Bishop of Meath is Premier Bishop of Ireland; they are Most
Reverend. So, too, is the Primus of Scotland, he being the senior
Scottish bishop. Before leaving the styles of bishops, it can be noted
that a few years ago the form of address for Roman Catholic
bishops was changed by Rome from My Lord to Excellency, but
that the former usage was retained in England to avoid confusion
with the normal title of diplomatic representatives sent to Britain.

Deans are the Very Reverend, eg, the Very Reverend the Dean
of Chichester. They may be addressed in speech as Mr Dean, also in
informal writing. The title of dean, like so many other ecclesiastical
styles, derives from a secular source, being merely *decanus*, one set
over ten. (Latin, cf Greek δέκα ten.) It was probably at one time
a military term, and was used in the early centuries of the Christian
era outside the religious sphere to denote various government
officials. It was brought into the ecclesiastical orbit when used of a
monk having the charge or supervision of ten other monks. As
cathedrals were frequently under the care of a body of monks, it
gradually became the custom for the *decanus* to be in control of the
cathedral. Sometimes he was under the authority of the *praepositus*,
or provost, but in the course of the later middle ages, deans took
the place of provosts. In the modern Church of England there are
only fourteen provosts as compared with twenty-nine deans of
cathedrals (in England).

Rural deans are a development of the time when archpriests were
put in charge of parts of a diocese to act in some respect on behalf
of the bishop. The rural dean in the Anglican Church has no special

style but is described, like any other clergyman, as the Reverend. The title of dean has found its way into secular usage again, for in the English universities one fellow of a college will generally hold the office of a dean, his concern being with discipline rather than teaching.

The archdeacon, as his name implies, was originally the chief of the deacons who were attached to a cathedral. From his close association with the bishop of his diocese, the archdeacon came to acquire very considerable powers. In the middle ages in Western Europe the archdeacon was really in control of the diocese and thus acquired great possibility of wealth and power. Resentment against what must have been the tyranny of archdeacons was expressed in the old tag, *Num archdiaconus possit salveri*; an archdeacon cannot be saved, can he? At the Reformation, the Council of Trent confined the power of the archdeacon to holding visitations in conjunction with the bishop, so that where the office still exists the function is restricted to the presentation of candidates for ordination. As for his other previous functions, these are now discharged by the Vicar General. The latter takes the place of the bishop, and carries out the latter's functions, except those which require episcopal consecration. The term Vicar General has also been used in a secular sense. Thus Thomas Cromwell was the Vicar General of Henry VIII, particularly in the work of dissolving the monasteries. It applies also to the chancellor of a diocese.

In the Anglican Church, the archdeacon is what might be termed the business manager of the diocese, acting on behalf of the bishop. He is styled the Venerable the Archdeacon of X, and in writing, Venerable Sir. 'Mr Archdeacon' is permissible in speech. Retired deans and provosts are styled, as with retired bishops, the Very Reverend Dean X; retired archdeacons are the Venerable Archdeacon X.

The title of canon is derived from the Greek Κανών, which means a straight rod or rule. It is applied to the principle by which the books of the Old and New Testament have been determined, hence the expression 'canonical scriptures'; also in secular writing, such phrases as 'canons of interpretation'. As applied to a clergyman, it comes from the ancient practice whereby a bishop lived a canonical life in common with his clergy who were caring for the cathedral. These clerics thus became the canons of the cathedral. They are now residential at a cathedral, but other honorary canons may be appointed, who do not have to reside there. The style of address of a canon in the Anglican Church is simply, the Reverend, in the Roman Church it is the Very Reverend. There is also the term 'priest vicar', which denotes a minor canon whose duty it is to sing the service.

A clerk in Holy Orders is described as the Reverend John Smith, etc. The use of the term Reverend must have originated after the Reformation, as no sign of it appears before that time. In England, it was a custom to call a priest, Sir John or Sir Thomas, and this practice persisted after the revolt against Rome, as readers of seventeenth-century literature will remember. In the case of clerics who possess a secular rank, the clerical title precedes it, thus the Reverend Lord Smith. In modern times in England, the Roman Catholic clergy and many Anglican clergy are addressed as 'Father'. Secular clergy should not be thus addressed, as the use of Father ought to be confined to the religious, ie, members of monastic or religious communities who are priests. I have heard it stated that the parochial Roman clergy were styled simply 'Mister' before the time of Cardinal Manning, himself a convert from Anglicanism to Catholicism. Priests and deacons are both termed Reverend. Occasionally one comes across a man who has taken deacon's orders in the Church of England but never been ordained priest. He is not as a rule addressed by a clerical title. Similarly, Anglican clergy who have resigned their orders under the Enabling Act, or who have joined the Church of Rome, are addressed as though they were laymen.

Next in importance among Christian bodies to the Catholic, Western, or Roman Catholic Church is the Orthodox Church. This is the vast organisation which has provided the religious faith of Russia, Greece, the other Balkan countries, Asia Minor, Armenia, Syria, Egypt etc. The organisation of the Orthodox Church differs from that of the Roman Church in that there is no central government of a Pope. There are four Patriarchates (the Orthodox regard the Pope as Patriarch of the West, having a primacy of honour among Patriarchs)—Constantinople, Alexandria, Antioch, Jerusalem —and the heads of these four bear the title of Patriarch. The titles of the four are as follows :

(i) Constantinople. His All Holiness Athenagoras I (or the name of the reigning pontiff), Archbishop of Constantinople, the New Rome, and Ecumenical Patriarch. He has a number of bishops under his jurisdiction and also some ecclesiastics called exarchs. The reader will recall that this name was given to those who ruled at Ravenna, another instance of the adoption by the church of secular titles. The exarchs rule over congregations which are outside the physical area contained in the Patriarchate. One of them rules over the Orthodox in Western Europe, has his seat in London, is an archbishop and is termed the Metropolitan. The Patriarch of Constantinople has his high place among the Orthodox Churches but has no authority over them. The very great position of this ecclesiastic is derived from the fact that his see was the imperial city, the seat of empire.

(ii) Alexandria. His Holiness, or His Divine Beatitude Christophoros II (the name of the Patriarch who died in July 1967), Pope and Patriarch of Alexandria, and All Africa, 13th Apostle and Judge of the Universe.

(iii) Antioch. His Holiness the Lord Alexander III, Patriarch of Antioch, the Great City of God, of Cilicia, of Iberia, of Syria, of Arabia and of all the East, Father of Fathers, Pastor of Pastors, 13th Apostle.

(iv) Jerusalem. His Holiness, or His Beatitude.

There are eleven other autocephalous churches : Russia, Rumania, Serbia (ie, in Yugoslavia), Greece, Bulgaria, Georgia, Cyprus, Czechoslovakia, Poland (this country is mainly Roman Catholic, the the only Slav nation to belong to the Latin church; it is estimated that there are some 350,000 Orthodox in Poland), Albania and Sinai. The heads of the Russian, Rumanian, Serbian and Bulgarian churches are styled His Holiness and Patriarch; the head of the Georgian church has the title of Catholicos Patriarch. The heads of other churches are called Archbishop, or Metropolitan.

There has been a change in the use of the latter term. Metropolitan formerly meant the bishop of the capital of a province. An archbishop was a bishop whose see was particularly eminent but not of necessity a provincial capital. The Russians still maintain this distinction but among the Greeks every bishop is styled a Metropolitan, while an archbishop presides over a province. The Metropolitan is styled His Beatitude.

Beside the Patriarchate of Alexandria, there is also the organisation of the Coptic or Egyptian Orthodox Church, with its Patriarch the Most Holy Father X, Patriarch of Alexandria, of all Egypt, of Nubia, Ethiopia, the Pentapolis, and all the country evangelised by St Mark. The head of the Ethiopian Church is His Beatitude the Abuna.

Monastic institutions are common to the Roman, the Orthodox and the Anglican Churches. In England before the Reformation, the mitred abbots of the great monasteries sat in the House of Lords. The head of a monastery is an abbot, and is styled My Lord Abbot, the Right Reverend Abbot of X or Right Reverend Father.

The head of a province in an order of monks is known as The Provincial and is addressed as Very Reverend Father. In some cases the term Dom (short for *Dominus*) is used before the names of monks.

In the Orthodox Church there are different titles as with Archimandrite, which meant a monk in charge of several monasteries, but now denotes a priest monk. The latter is named Hieromonk in Greek, a priest monk. The abbot of a monastery is the Higumenos. The head of a monastery is also styled the Superior or, in the case of a priory (which ranks below an abbey), the Prior.

Although with very few exceptions, and these in some of the Protestant churches, women have not been admitted to the Christian ministry, there have from early times been many orders of women in the church. There was undoubtedly an order of deaconesses in the early church, whose principal duties were to assist those of their own sex who were sick or in trouble. This order was revived in the Church of England in 1862.

Orders of the religious life for women abound. The head of a nunnery is the Mother Superior, the Reverend Mother. The nuns are called Sisters, and are addressed as Sister Mary etc, according to the Christian name taken when they made their profession of the final vows.

In Scotland, the Church is presbyterian and is established. The leader of this church is the Moderator and is entitled The Right Reverend the Moderator of the General Assembly of the Church of Scotland. A former Moderator is the Very Reverend. The Queen is represented by the Lord High Commissioner, whose style is His Grace the Lord High Commissioner, the Right Honourable John Smith, and otherwise as for a duke. The Dean of the Thistle and Chapel Royal in St Giles' Cathedral, Edinburgh, is addressed like an Anglican dean. Otherwise, the clergy of the Established Church of Scotland are given the title of Reverend, as with their nonconforming brethren of the Episcopal Church in Scotland. In fact, Reverend is an ubiquitous title for it now used by, and about, the ministers of all the denominations. In former generations, the ministers of the English Noncomformist bodies were known simply as Mister, and their conventicles as chapels. Now, as the latter have become churches, so their ministers are called the Reverend, resultting in awkward confusion as to whether a particular reverend gentleman belongs to the Anglican, Roman Catholic, or Free Church bodies. Incidentally, the Roman Catholics are as much a Nonconformist body as are the Baptists or Wesleyans, and all alike who did not assent to the Established Church were formerly subject to legal disabilities. On this matter there was an instructive article in the 1951 (and only) edition of *Who's Who in the Free Churches*, by Francis Cowper.

The head of British Jewry is the Chief Rabbi. He bears the title of the Very Reverend the Chief Rabbi. Jewish rabbis in general are addressed as The Reverend Rabbi J. Smith.

14. From China to Ireland

It would be inappropriate to conclude this sketch without making some slight reference to the great state whose existence is unique in the world's history—China, the only country which can show a continuous record from a time contemporary with the Pharaohs until the present day. The history of China resembles the course of some of her greatest rivers: at one time flowing in order and bringing prosperity, at others subject to no restraint and spreading devastation and ruin over the land. A period of anarchy followed by the rise of a strong dynasty, which brings peace, prosperity and conquest over the foreigner, until that dynasty exhibits the unfailing decadence which attends most royal families—such has been the story of China from nearly 2,000 years BC until the twentieth century.

The pattern has always been the same. After a time of weakness of the central government, with the consequent rise of petty tyrants, one of the more forceful and energetic of the lords has at last made himself the master of China, ascended the Dragon Throne, and become the Son of Heaven, almost as if he had succeeded the last emperor of the former dynasty by right divine. This process should have been repeated after the fall of the Manchu dynasty in 1912, when the power in China seemed, as in former ages, to be in the hands of one man. Yuan Shih Kai ousted the reformer Sun Yat Sen from the presidency of the new republic and prepared to elevate himself to the imperial throne as the new Son of Heaven. Then, for the first time, the age-old pattern of Chinese history was disrupted; new forces had appeared and there was a break with the past. No new royal dynasty was to arise. The era of internal dissension seemed to have returned, the vassals of China threw off the yoke, and the Japanese renewed much more vigorously the onslaught they had first made in the sixteenth century. The rest is well known. Nationalism, combined with recurrent economic difficulties, caused a break with the traditional past. After a period of intense trouble,

160

China was unified once more, but this time by the Communist leader, Mao Tse-tung. An entirely new regime began with the acceptance of the philosophy of Karl Marx as a leading principle. Strange tale! A German Jew, exiled from Germany, studies and writes in London, lives and dies in poverty and then in the next century his principles triumph in Russia and China.

In the modern China it appears that almost everything out of the past is regarded as useless. No such thing as a title beyond the humble and delusive 'comrade' is allowed. The whole elaborate apparatus of the old imperial system has gone beyond recall, even in memory. We can, therefore, only mention the titled system as it once was. Probably few titles of foreign origin have so embedded themselves in English usage as that of 'mandarin', which is not a Chinese title, though it refers to Chinese officials, either civil or military, who were graded as all officials are in any country. The word is derived from a Malay term, *mantri*, denoting a counsellor or minister, and reached Europe through Portuguese. A reference to a mandarin, apart from historical usage, is almost always pejorative, implying an adherence to rules employed without thought or feeling.

European accounts of Chinese history refer constantly to emperors, princes and dukes. According to some accounts, the Chinese under the emperors possessed other ranks of nobility equivalent to those of Europe. Thus a duke was *koong*, a marquess *how*, an earl *paak*, a baron *tze* and even a baronet, *nan*, possessed an identity in the Chinese scale of hereditary honours. These nobles were divided into classes, at first glance rather like the degrees of precedence among our peers, though in fact the Chinese principle was quite different. Class among the nobles depended upon the number of generations through which the title was allowed to be inherited. Some dukedoms could be inherited in the male line for twenty-six, twenty-five or twenty-four generations. The proudest pedigrees of Europe would have to cede place to descents of this length, but it must be remembered that the system of ancestor worship provided a powerful incentive to the maintenance of genealogical record, and to the begetting of male heirs. Pedigrees of the descendants of Confucius are known which extend over 2,500 years.

Additional to these five classes of nobility were two other ranks, *Kee-Too-Wye* and *Wan-Kee-Wye*, with inheritance for a lesser number of generations. Many other degrees of rank existed, classified as *Ching*, correct and *Tsung*, deputy. Nearly all upper-class occupations came under one of these two headings and an elaborate system was maintained to cover all the exigencies of social calls when an inferior had to visit a superior in rank. In fact, the colloquial English expression about servile behaviour, 'bowing and scraping', had a literal meaning in imperial China. 'A military mandarin of the third rank when visiting a military mandarin of the first rank wears armour, and on entering the visitors' hall kneels and knocks his head upon the ground three times. He then rises and makes three profound bows, which his superior officer acknowledges by three half bows.' (*China*, by J. H. Gray, Archdeacon of Hongkong, 1878, vol i, p 353.) Our western military salute seems more useful and much simpler.

The Chinese system makes that of old Byzantium, its nearest analogue, appear almost easy going and informal, though in many respects it had a logicality of its own. Thus a father was allowed to take a title of equal rank when one had been conferred upon his son; the principle of ancestor worship was in this way not impaired, for how could a man pay proper respect to a shade whose rank had been lower than his own? Honours were often given to the dead in consequence of the advancement of the living, and in some cases mandarins could confer titles on their fathers. Although the official grades (as distinct from nobility) were not inheritable, a man's advancement in title could be influenced by the rank of his deceased father. Women generally took the ranks and titles of their husbands, at least the first wife did.

The Nobles of Malta. These are possessed of titles of nobility which go back to the year 1090, the time of Count Roger the Norman, who then drove the Moslems from Malta. When the island was granted by the Emperor Charles V to the Knights of St John of Jerusalem in 1530, the Grand Master confirmed the rights and privileges of the Maltese nobility. The same confirmation was given by the British government when it took possession of the island. The Maltese nobility consists of nine marquisates, ten countships, and ten baronies. The nobles are officially addressed as Most Noble; the eldest sons are styled *Marchesino, Contino,* or *Baroncino,* and the younger sons and the daughters are styled *dei Marchesi, dei Conti,* or *dei Baroni*. The premier noble of Malta is the Baron of Diar-Il-Bniet and Bukana, and Baron of Castel Cicciano. These are titles heritable through the female line.

162

The Seigneurs of Canada. When the British won Canada from the French, they recognized the rights of certain seigneurs in that country. The most prominent of these is the Baron de Longueuil, of Longueuil in the province of Quebec, created by Louis XIV on 26 January 1700, with remainder to descendants, male and female or by tenure. The title was recognised by Queen Victoria on 4 December 1880.

Highland Chiefs. Often someone asks: 'Is it correct to refer to a Highland chief as The Mackintosh, or The Macpherson?' The answer is 'Yes', with certain additional information for elucidation. Feudal usages linger very much in Scotland. The style given by Sir Walter Scott in *Waverley* to the old gentleman who had been 'out' in both the 1715 and 1745 rebellions, was that of Baron of Bradwardine, though to English folk he would have appeared as untitled. The difference is explained by the fact that Bradwardine (the fictitious can take the place of the real) was a feudal barony. Its owner was, therefore, correctly termed a baron, but he was not a peer or lord of Parliament, the term by which Scots writers designated our barons, viscounts etc. Just as Bradwardine took his surname from his property, so he was correctly referred to as Bradwardine. To have used 'Mr' would have been incorrect. In documents, he would have been either the Laird of Bradwardine, or Bradwardine of that ilk. The latter expression is common in Scots literature to describe a person whose surname and property name are identical, and also indicates that he is the chief of the line. It is used of lowland lairds and highland chiefs alike. The title of baron is now correctly used even by those who have not inherited any lands to accompany it. Madame is the style used for the wife of a Scots feudal baron (and also the Lady of X). The wives and unmarried daughters of chiefs, chieftains and lairds are entitled to use the styles or Mrs Udny of Udny etc. (*The Clans, Septs and Regiments of the Scottish Highlands*, by Frank Adam, sixth edition, revised by Sir Thomas Innes of Learney, 1960, p 408.) The heir to the lairdship is described as the Younger, eg, Pirie Gordon the Younger of Buthlaw; or Mackintosh of that ilk; Mrs Mackintosh of that ilk; Ian Mackintosh, younger of that ilk; and the sister of the last named, Miss Jean Mackintosh of Mackintosh. The younger sons do not bear these titles, as they will probably found families and houses of their own.

Ambassadors and Diplomats. Ambassadors are addressed as His

Excellency the Ambassador Extraordinary and Plenipotentiary of the Republic, eg, of France; British ambassadors to foreign states are styled His Excellency Her Britannic Majesty's Ambassador Extraordinary and Minister Plenipotentiary to the Republic of France. An Envoy Extraordinary etc, is addressed in accordance with his rank as Her Britannic Majesty's Evoy etc. Similarly, a Minister Resident, but neither he nor the envoy are called Excellency. So, too, with consuls, vice-consuls, consuls general, and agents, John Smith, Esq, HBM Consul etc.

The titles and precedence of the Diplomatic Corps have been evolved after much argument and some bloodshed. An ambassador to the Court of St James (note the accrediting is to the old court of the sovereign) cannot be arrested or pursued by writs or legal process in either a civil or criminal cause. Similar immunity is accorded by English law to his staff and to his domestic servants (provided the latter are registered as Embassy servants with one of Her Majesty's Principal Secretaries of State), though not to persons trading with him. The courts of this country cannot entertain a suit against a diplomat, eg, for breach of promise, unless his government gives permission for him to defend the action. It is, of course, open to a government to request the removal from an embassy of an ambassador or member of his staff whom that government considers undesirable. It is possible that in the event of a grave act of treason, such as an attempt on the sovereign's life, even the most civilized state would put diplomatic immunity aside, but such an act is almost inconceivable and generally the diplomat's immunity is a sure and certain defence around him. Lawyers sum it up under the harsh term 'extraterritoriality', which means that Grosvenor Square is Little America.

The punctilios of diplomatic life are of extreme nicety. The regulations of HM Foreign Service fill nearly forty closely-printed pages in a volume of over 500. The uniforms to be worn, the flags to be flown by diplomatic and consular agents, the salutes of guns to be accorded the various ranks of diplomats, are all matters of carefully arranged gradation. The British regulations correspond with similar regulations in foreign states. Any change in precedence among those accredited to the Court of St James's is a matter for very serious consultation between the governments concerned. One of the post-war changes was that in the precedence of Commonwealth High Commissioners. Their position in the table of precedence was formerly far down, below a baron or a secretary of state who was a commoner. Now High Commissioners rank with ambassadors of foreign states immediately after the Lord Privy Seal, in a common order of seniority based on their respective dates of arrival in the United Kingdom for the purpose of assuming their official duties. The High Commissioners are also given the title of Excellency. The arrangement about the ranking of ambassadors corresponds to the equally simple protocol by which signatories to a treaty sign in the alphabetical order of their countries' names.

Although ambassadorial functions are of an extreme antiquity, the modern *corps diplomatique* is of comparatively recent origin. The *bon mot* of a Viennese lady describing (about 1754) the numerous foreign representatives in her city, the term has now become officially adopted here and all over the world. The words 'diplomacy' and 'diplomat' are much older, being derived from the Greek 'diploma', the duplicate or copy of an act emanating from the sovereign of which the original is retained. Hence the word diplomatics or diplomatology as applied to the study of historical documents of an official nature.

The establishment of permanent embassies in Europe was slow to develop, the Duke of Milan having been the first prince to establish such a permanent representation at Genoa in 1455. It was natural for the Italian states to be the pioneers of diplomacy. The numerous petty sovereignties of Italy were constantly at war or trading with each other, and as they shared a common language and way of life they soon built up, especially the Venetians and Genoese, a diplomatic service. Gradually the process spread throughout Europe. The oldest permanent representation in England is that of Spain, which has been almost continuous since 1487. The first Venetian ambassador to visit England came in 1319 to demand compensation for injury to Venetian commerce by English pirates, but the representation was not kept up. The establishment of regular embassies throughout Europe and other civilized areas of the world dates from the seventeenth and eighteenth centuries. England was slow to build up her foreign service, despite her world-wide trade and interests. For centuries the sovereign had only two principal secretaries of state, and in the eighteenth century these were responsible for the northern and southern divisions of the globe. In 1782 they evolved into Home Secretary (with responsibility for Ireland) and

165

the Foreign Secretary, of which post Fox may be considered the first holder.

The establishment of the Foreign Office continued to be for many decades miserly, a couple of dozen clerks occupying dingy offices. The staff was recruited, however, from noble and distinguished families, although for security reasons much of their work consisted in copying important documents by hand. Salaries were extremely low and it was not until Edward VII's reign that the qualification of a private income of £400 a year ceased to be necessary. In the Cockpit in Whitehall Gardens, and later in Downing Street, working conditions were very bad. On one occasion a dead cat was found behind a series of bound volumes on a shelf. The body was sent up in a despatch case to Lord John Russell, then Foreign Secretary, and by him passed around the Cabinet for inspection. Presumably this noisome incident had some influence on events, for in 1868 Sir Gilbert Scott built the present Foreign Office. In 1889 the first typist was introduced, to relieve the tedium of laborious hand copying, and entry to the service was made dependent on examination. The Foreign Office List was begun by Sir Edward Hertslet. In the last war while the Earl of Avon (then Anthony Eden) was Foreign Secretary, the Foreign Office staff was amalgamated with the diplomatic and consular service under the title of Her Majesty's Foreign Service.

The Foreign Secretary deals with all representations to foreign powers whether in or out of this country. An ambassador has right of audience with a sovereign or head of state, and the representative of a foreign power must present his credentials to Her Majesty in person. This does not necessarily coincide with the ambassador's arrival in this country and, in practice, some considerable time may elapse before the audience with Her Majesty takes place. The British Diplomatic Corps is headed by a Marshal, with a Vice-Marshal and an Assistant Marshal. They are listed as members of the royal household, but the Vice-Marshal is also a member of the Foreign Service. His function is to deal with protocol, ie, the etiquette relating to diplomats, such as their order of seating at a dinner.

The Foreign Secretary grants interviews to foreign ambassadors and summons them to interview when necessary. All their representations regarding their governments must be made through him. The immunity which they enjoy from legal process is governed by an Act of Parliament of 1708 which was caused, curiously enough, by the arrest of the Russian ambassador by certain private persons. The preamble to the statute relates how 'several turbulent and disorderly persons in a most outrageous manner insulted the person of His Excellency Andrew Artemonowitz Matueof, Ambassador Extraordinary of His Czarish Majesty, Emperor of Great Russia, Her Majesty's good friend and ally, by arresting him and taking him by violence out of his coach in the public street, and detaining him in custody for several hours.'

The diplomatic bag is immune as well as the diplomatic person, and for centuries the ambassador was looked upon as an honourable spy. Sir Henry Wotten, Provost of Eton and platonic lover of Elizabeth of Bohemia, himself Ambassador of England in various foreign states, defined the duties of the diplomat in the famous words : 'An ambassador is an honest man sent to lie abroad for his country.' Indeed a writer of romance like Harrison Ainsworth, with his Spanish and French ambassadors plotting away the lives and liberties of Englishmen, imagined no more than what was actually attempted by the Austrian and German ministers to the USA during the first world war. In the last war, German embassies in neutral countries were centres of espionage against the Allies. For instance, as one stood on the airfield at Gibraltar one could see German agents on the roof of their house in Spain watching the movements of our aircraft. Indeed it is said that one British controller who thought an aircraft overdue telephoned the Germans and got the correct details from them.

The Treaty of Vienna (1815) established the regulations governing the ranks of diplomatic agents. They were then grouped as ambassadors, legates, or nuncios; envoys or ministers accredited to sovereigns; and chargés d'affaires accredited to Foreign Ministers. The period since the last war has seen a very great growth in the conversion of legations into embassies.

The immunity enjoyed by ambassadors was won after long eras of uncivilised conduct. Instances abound in ancient history of the bad treatment of envoys and of their bad behaviour. In medieval times, there was a class of men, the heralds, whose persons were considered sacred, and who therefore, before the rise of the *corps diplomatique*, often undertook ambassadorial duties.

Officers of Arms. Very few countries now maintain heralds as such. England, Scotland, the Republic of Ireland, Spain, Sweden, Denmark and the Republic of South Africa are those which occur to

167

my memory. It is often stated that Switzerland possesses state heralds but the Swiss authorities have informed me that this is not so. In England, matters heraldic are controlled by the Earl Marshal, an office of state hereditary in the family of Howard, in the person of the reigning Duke of Norfolk. The thirteen officers under his jurisdiction form the College of Arms, or Heralds, and are members of the Queen's household. The officers are (i) three Kings of Arms; Garter, Clarenceaux and Norroy; (ii) six Heralds: Chester, Lancaster, Richmond, Somerset, Windsor and York; (iii) four Pursuivants, or junior Heralds, the word Pursuivant meaning follower: Bluemantle, Portcullis, Rouge Croix, and Rogue Dragon. All these officers are addressed by their respective rank, civil or military. I have given at length an account of the origin of these medieval-style titles in my book, *The Story of Heraldry*.

In Scotland, the authority is the Lord Lyon, who is the equivalent of the Earl Marshal in England. His style is the Rt Hon Sir Thomas Innes of Learney, KCVO, Lord Lyon King of Arms. The present holder is a laird and therefore 'of Learney', the name of his estate; a Lyon who was landless would still be the Rt Hon the Lord Lyon King of Arms, and almost certainly a knight. The Scottish Heralds are Albany and Marchmount; the Pursuivants, Kintyre, Unicorn and Carrick. In both England and Scotland, Officers Extraordinary (Heralds usually in the former, Pursuivants in the latter country) are sometimes appointed. The Lord Lyon is a judge of the Court of Session. As the Scottish legal system was maintained at the Union with England in 1707, Scottish heraldry continued as a separate jurisdiction.

In Ireland, there was formerly the office of Ulster King of Arms, the equivalent of the English and Scottish chief officers. This was withdrawn from Dublin Castle and united with the office of Norroy. In its place the Republican Government appointed its own Chief Herald of Ireland. In Sweden, the chief herald is the Chamberlain to the King. In South Africa, a State Herald was appointed under The Heraldry Act (No 18, 1962).

Ministers of the British Government. The Prime Minister is styled the Right Honourable (Sir) John Smith, according to his rank as a private person, Prime Minister and First Lord of the Treasury. The latter post reflects the fact that, until 1905, the Prime Minister was unknown to the constitution and to the Table of Precedence, and held the position of First Lord of the Treasury in order to give him an official existence and place. Cabinet Ministers have Right Honourable before their names and Ministers not in the Cabinet are also styled thus, but not junior Ministers unless they are Privy Counsellors. Right Honourable is used before the names of the latter but in that case the letters PC are not given after the name. In Canada, members of the Privy Council bear the title of Honourable for life, and so do members of the Executive Councils of Australia, and of the states of Victoria and Tasmania. In various other Dominion states, tenure of ministerial and senatorial office confers the title of Honourable on retirement.

Civic Dignitaries. It is impossible within the space available to cover these titles throughout Europe, but in English-reading countries the following will be of interest. The mayor of an English city is The Right Worshipful. The mayor of a borough is the Worshipful. There are eighteen Lord Mayors in England and Wales; three in Ireland. They are styled the Right Honourable the Lord Mayor. In Scotland, the Lord Provost is the equivalent of the Lord Mayor, and the Provost of Mayor. There are six Lord Provosts, of Edinburgh, Aberdeen, Glasgow, Dundee, Elgin and Perth, of which only Edinburgh and Glasgow have a Lord Provost entitled to the Rt Hon before their names. The Chairman of the Greater London Council is the Right Honourable.

Dignitaries of the Law. The Right Honourable the Lord High Chancellor of Great Britain is the head of the legal profession. The Attorney-General and the Solicitor-General are the Right Honourable and are knighted on appointment. The Lord Chief Justice is the Right Honourable. A Lord Justice of Appeal is the Right Honourable Lord Justice. Judges of the High Court are the Honourable Mr Justice, are always knighted, and while on the Bench are addressed as My Lord, or Your Lordship. The Master of the Rolls (the judge who is in charge of the Public Record Office) is : the Right Honourable the Master of the Rolls. He is usually a peer, so that rank would follow Rt Hon. Justices of the Peace are Your Worship (on the Bench) and the Right Worshipful in highly formal letters; they have the letters 'JP' after their names.

The Lord Lieutenant of the county is Her Majesty's Lieutenant of Sussex, followed by his rank, very often that of a peer. A DL is a Deputy Lieutenant. In the Scottish legal system, the Lord Advocate, a political appointee, is the Right Honourable (only while in office, unless he is a Privy Councillor). The Judges of the Court of Session,

169

the Lords of Sessions, are fourteen in number; the Lord President and Lord Justice General, and the Lord Justice Clerk are both Right Honourable, and twelve other judges who are styled the Honourable Lord X. This title of Lord is kept on retirement and the judges' wife is Lady, the style being exactly the same as that of a baron.

In the Dominions, the style of Honourable is used for judges of the High Court of Australia, of the Supreme Courts of New South Wales, Victoria, Queensland, South Australia, Western Australia, Tasmania, New Zealand (and of South Africa); of the Supreme and Exchequer Courts of Canada, and of certain courts in Canadian Provinces. In some cases the prefix may be retained after retirement.

Irish Chiefs. Much the same system prevailed among the Celts of Ireland as with their brethren of the Highlands of Scotland. There are about seventy chieftainships in Ireland and these are being carefully studied by the office of the Chief Herald of Ireland. Some of them have been officially recorded. Famous instances are those of The O'Conor Don, whose ancestors were High Kings of Ireland when it was invaded by the Anglo-Normans in 1168-1172. The O'Donovan, the O'Kelley; the Maelseachlain (Anglicised or Scotised as the McLoughlin) whose ancestry goes back to a renowned chief who died about AD 405, Niall of the Nine Hostages, are some of the most renowned of the great native houses of Ireland. The four provinces of Ireland—Ulster, Munster, Leinster and Connaught—were anciently ruled by dynasties of kings, and among these the one who was the most powerful, and who could establish his right by making the circuit of Ireland, was known as the High King, or Ard Righ.*

At the end of this study I am led to muse on the peculiarity in our nature which brings human beings to devise titles for themselves; and on the fact that this is a persistent trait in the history of nations. No really equalitarian society has yet appeared. However it may have aspired to equality, it has rapidly developed the ability to make some of its members more equal than others; an observation as applicable to the USSR as to Napoleonic France. It may,

---

*Another Celtic island, that of Man, had a peculiar history, being ruled in turn by Norse, Scots and English kings, the last of these being appointed by the English Crown. Thirteen members of the Stanley family, the Earls of Derby, were Kings of Man. It was not until after the Restoration in 1660 that their dominion passed to the British Crown.

170

therefore, be assumed that titular distinctions will always be with us. That hereditary titles will disappear or cease to be created is an equal certainty. Against them there is a decided animus in the modern world.

When, according to Christian doctrine, the Deity appeared among men, He came not as a great monarch or noble, but as a plain man and an artisan. The example of the God Man, the Carpenter of Nazareth, has not been conspicuously followed by His adherents. Pride was the cause of Lucifer's fall and he has succeeded in infecting even the children of light with the master sin. Right up to the last trumpet, the subject of modes of address will affect and afflict humanity. Very few men or women are in all honesty uninterested in honorific distinctions.

Index